A Tapestry of Motivational and Inspirational Thoughts

Selected by
Louise and Ivin Holt
Provo, Utah
2009

TABLE OF CONTENTS
For Volume II

Section   Page

11. Mother's and Father's Influence 1
12. Freedom, Justice, Patriotism, Liberty 33
13. Happiness, Friendship, Kindness 49
14. Life, Talents, Time, Values 87
15. Love, Sharing, Service, Sacrifice 121
16. Choices, Thoughts, Actions, Sorrow 149
17. Teacher, Teaching, Education 169
18. Forgiving, Tolerance, Mercy, Greed 189
19. Work, Responsibility, Leisure, Idleness, Debt . . 203
20. Smiles, Laughter, Hugs, Humor 229

                       Index begins on page   257

ACKNOWLEDGMENT

We express our sincere thanks to the known authors a nd the unknown authors which we were unable to locate. These many authors have truly left their foot prints in the sands of time. The compilers chose the selected quotes, poems and stories because of their power to not only inspire and uplift the human heart but to give cheer and encouragement to the discouraged and downtrodden. The lighthearted messages can move one from t ears to smiles and laughter and brighten the hearts of the weary.

Reasonable e ffort has been made to trace the ownership of the copyrighted material. We acknowledge the possibility of inadvertent omissions of due credit. In the event of questions arising as to the use of articles, in future editions, if any, necessary corrections where possible will be made. We acknowledge the many great authors whose selections are in the public domain.

We express thanks to friends and family for their encouragement in completing this undertaking.

To the following publishers, authors, or agents, we express thanks for granting permission to reprint previously published materials.

If Jesus Came to Your House by Lois Eades. Copyright c Beacon Hill Press of Kansas City, Kansas City, Missouri. Used by permission of the publisher. All rights reserved.
Excerpt from the book, *Children Learn What They Live.* copyright 1998 by Dorothy Law Nolte and Rachael Harris. T he Poem "*Children Learn What They Live*" on page vi, Copyright c 1972 by Dorothy Law Nolte. Used by permission of Workman Publishing Co., Inc., New York. All Rights Reserved.
Quote of the John D. Rockefeller, Jr. *Credo.* Used by permission of David Strawbridge, G eneral Counsel of the Rockefeller Family Office. New York, N.Y.

Mother's and Father's Influence

Section 11

Train up a child in the way he should go:
And when he is old,
He will not depart from it.
Proverbs 22:6

Mother's and Father's Influence

Mother's Face

Three little boys talked together
One sunny summer day
And I leaned out the window
To hear what they had to say;

"The prettiest thing I ever saw,"
One of the little boys said,
"Was a bird in grandma's garden,
All black and white and red."

"The prettiest thing I ever saw,"
Said the second little lad,
"Was a pony at a circus–
I wanted him awfully bad."

"I think," said the third little fellow,
With a grave and gentle face,
"That the prettiest thing in all the world,
Is just my mother's face."
—*Author Unknown*

My mother gave to me–
everything money can not buy.
—*Author Unknown*

Only One Mother

Hundreds of stars in the pretty sky;
Hundreds of shells on the shore together,
Hundreds of birds that go singing by,
Hundreds of dew-drops to greet the dawn,
Hundreds of bees in the purple clover,
Hundreds of butterflies on the lawn,
But only one Mother the wide world over.
—*Author Unknown*

When Mother's There

When Mother's anywhere around,
Or so it seems to me,
It makes a lot of difference,
With most everything you see.

No matter if the night is dark,
With shadows everywhere,
I'm not a single bit afraid,
So long as Mother's there.

For when I hear my mother's voice,
And see her smile so bright,
No matter what has happened,
Then everything's all right.
—*Author Unknown*

Mother's and Father's Influence

The mother in her office holds the key of the soul; and she it is who stamps the coin of character.
—Author Unknown

I attribute all my success in life to the moral, intellectual, and physical education which I have received from my mother.
—George Washington

All that I am or hope to be I owe to my angel mother.
—Abraham Lincoln

My mother was the making of me. She was so true, so sure of me, that I felt I had someone to live for, someone I must not disappoint.
—Thomas Edison

In 1914, President Woodrow Wilson asked that the American flag be put out on every government building on the second Sunday of May every year thus setting aside that day as Mother's Day.

A Prayer

Father I thank Thee for my Mother,
And for the love that's like no other.
For her dear thought and loving care,
That makes our lives so sweet and fair,
Help us to love her as we should,
To prove our love by being good,
In all we do, in work and play,
To make each day a
Mother's Day.
—Author Unknown

What Matters

My mother says, she doesn't care
About the color of my hair,
Nor if my eyes are blue or brown,
Nor if my nose turns up or down
It really doesn't matter.

But if I cheat or tell a lie
Or say mean things to make folks cry,
Or if I'm rude or impolite
And do not try to do the right
That's what really matters.
—Author unknown

Mother's and Father's Influence

Which Loved Best

"I love you, mother," said little John;
Then forgetting his work, his cap went on,
And he was off to the garden swing,
Leaving his mother the wood to bring.

"I love you, mother," said rosy Nell;
"I love you better than tongue can tell;"
Then she teased and pouted full half the day,
Till her mother rejoiced when she went to play.

"I love you, mother," said little Fan
"Today I'll help you all I can;
How glad I am that school doesn't keep!"
So she rocked the baby till it fell asleep.

Then, stepping softly, she took the broom,
And swept the floor, and dusted the room;
Busy and happy all day long was she,
Helpful and cheerful as child could be.

"I love you, mother," again they said–
Three little children going to bed;
How do you think that mother guessed
Which of them really loved her best?
  –Joy Allison

Mother's and Father's Influence

Send Them To Bed With A Kiss

O Mother, so weary, discouraged,
Worn out with the cares of the day,
You often grow cross and impatient,
Complain of the noise and the play;
For the day brings so many vexations,
   So many things going amiss;
But, mothers, whatever may vex you;
   Send the children
      to bed with a kiss!

The dear little feet wonder often. . .
Perhaps, from the pathway of right.
The dear little hands find new mischief
To try you from morning till night;
But think of the desolate mothers
Who'd give all the worlds for your bliss,
And, as thanks for your infinite blessings,
   Send the children
      to bed with a kiss!

For some day their noise will not vex you,
   The silence will hurt you far more;
You will long for their sweet childish voices,
   For a sweet childish face at the door;
And to press a child's face to your bosom,
   You'd give all the world for just this!
For the comfort 'twill bring you in sorrow,
   Send the children
      to bed with a kiss!
         –In New Orleans Picayune

Mother's and Father's Influence

Mother's Boys

Yes, I know there are stains on my carpet,
   The traces of small muddy boots;
And I see your fair tapestry glowing,
   All spotless with flowers and fruits.

I know that my walls are disfigured
   With prints of small fingers and hands;
And that your own household most truly
   In immaculate purity stands.

And I know that my parlor is littered
   With many odd treasures and toys,
While your own is in daintiest order,
   Unharmed by the presence of boys.

And I know that my room is invaded
   Quite boldly all hours of the day,
While you sit in yours unmolested,
   And dream the soft quiet away.

Yes, I know there are four little bedsides
   Where I must stand watchful each night,
While you may go out in your carriage
   And flash in your dresses so bright.

Now, I think I'm a neat little woman;
   And I like my house orderly, too;
And I'm fond of all dainty belongings,
   Yet I would not change places with you.

No! Keep your fair home with its order,
   Its freedom from bother and noise;
And keep your own fanciful leisure,
   But give me my four splendid boys.
         —Author Unknown

Mother's and Father's Influence

To My Mother

I see her in her rocking chair
When day's long work is done.
I visualize her beauty rare,
I know the love she's won.
I see the toil of months and years
Well worn now in her brow.
I see her calming all my fears
I see it plainly now.

I marvel at her tender love,
And at her gracious care.
I kneel before the throne above
To give this humble prayer:

Take care of Mother dear,
And bless her in thy sight
For on thy righteous path she'd trod
To bask in gospel light.

She's taught each daughter and each son
To love and honor thee,
A great reward she's rightly won
For all eternity.

And so, dear Father, in thy Son's name
I humbly ask tonight,
That thou wilt keep alive the flame
Of Mother's shining light;
To send it forth through all the earth,
To spread thy truths again.
For all these things of priceless worth
I thank thee, Father;
Amen.

–Naomi Johnstone

Mother's and Father's Influence

What Is Home Without A Mother

What is home without a mother?
What are all the loving joys we meet?
When her loving smile no longer
Greets the coming of our feet.
The days seem long, the nights seem drear,
And time rolls slowly on,
And, oh! how few are childhood's pleasures
When her gentle care is gone.

Things we prize are first to vanish,
Hearts we love to pass away;
And how soon, e'en in our childhood,
We behold her turning gray;
Her eye grows dim, her step is slow;
Her joys of earth are past;
And sometimes ere we learn to know her,
She hath breathed on earth her last.

Older hearts may have their sorrows,
Grief that quickly die away,
But a mother lost in childhood,
Grieves the heart from day to day;
We miss her kind, her willing hand,
Her fond and honest care;
And, oh, how dark is life around us!
What is home without her care?
–*Alice Hawthorne*

Mother's and Father's Influence

The Bravest Battle

The bravest battle that ever was fought,
  Shall I tell you where and when?
On the maps of the world you will find it not,
  "Twas fought by the mothers of men.

  Nay, not with a cannon or battle shot,
    With sword or noble pen,
  Nay, not with eloquent words or thought
    From mouths of wonderful men.

    But deep in a woman's walled-up heart-
      Of woman that would not yield,
    But patiently, silently bore her part-
      Lo, there was the battle-field.

  No marshalling troops, no bivouac song
    No banner to gleam and wave,
  But, O, these battles they last so long,
    From babyhood to the grave!

Yet faithful still as a bridge of stars
  She fights in her walled-up town-
Fights on and on in the endless wars,
  Then silent, unseen-goes down.

  O ye with banners and battle shot,
    And soldiers to shout and praise,
  I tell you that kingliest victories brought
    Were fought in these silent ways.

    O spotless woman in a world of shame,
      With splendid and silent scorn,
    Go back to God as white as you came
      The kingliest warrior born.
          –*Joaquin Miller*

Mother's and Father's Influence

Memory

I stood and watched him playing,
   A little lad of three,
And back to me came straying
   The years that used to be;
In him the boy was Maying
   Who once belonged to me.

The selfsame brown his eyes were
   As those that once I knew;
As glad and gay his cries were,
   He owned his laughter too.
His features, form and size were
   My baby's, through and through.

His ears were those I'd sung to;
   His chubby little hands
Were those that I had clung to;
   His hair in golden strands
It seemed my heart was strung to
   By love's unbroken bands.

With him I lived the old days
   That seem so far away;
The beautiful and bold days
   When he was here to play;
The sunny and the gold days
   Of that remembered May.

I know not who he may be
   Nor where his home may be,
But I shall every day be
   In hope again to see
The image of the baby
   Who once belonged to me.

–Author Unknown

Mother's and Father's Influence

Somebody's Mother

The woman was old, and ragged and gray
And bent with the chill of the winter days,
The street was wet with the recent snow,
And the woman's feet were aged and slow.

She stood at the crossing and waited long,
Alone, uncared-for amid the throng
Of human beings that passed her by,
Not heeding the glance of her anxious eye.

Down the street with laugh and shout,
Glad in the freedom of "school let out,"
Came the boys like a flock of sheep,
Finding the snow piled white and deep.

Past the old woman, so old and gray,
Hastened the children on their way,
Nor offering a helping hand to her,
So meek, so timid, afraid to stir.

Lest the carriage wheels or the horses' feet
Should crowd her down in the slippery street;
At last came out of the merry troop
The happiest, kindest lad of the group.

He paused beside her and whispered low,
I'll help you across, if you wish to go."
Her aged hand on his strong young arm
She placed, and without hurt or harm

He guided the trembling feet along,
Proud that his own were firm and strong;
Then back again to his friends he went,
His young heart happy and well content.

Mother's and Father's Influence

"She's somebody's mother, boys, you know,
For all she's aged, and poor, and slow,
And I hope some fellow will lend a hand,
To help my mother, you understand,

"If ever she's poor and old and gray,
When her own dear boy is far away!"
And somebody's mother bowed her head
In her home that night, and she prayed,
She said, "God be kind to that noble boy
Who was somebody's son, and pride, and joy."
–*Author unknown*

I Wish I Had The Power To Write

I wish I had the power to write
The thoughts within my heart tonight.
As I sit and watch the lonely stars,
And wonder how and where you are.
You know, Mom, it's a funny thing,
How close, a son, a mission can bring;
And how for months now I've tried
To keep my emotions deep inside.
I told you brave men never cry–
I'm sorry, Mom I guess I lied.
For if we stood here to embrace,
You'd find a tear stain on my face.
I'm sorry if when I was home,
I left you standing all alone.
For it was you who shared my fears,
And soothed my hurt and dried my tears.
Yes, if I had the power to write,
The things within my heart tonight,
The words would ring out loud and true,
I'm proud to say, "Mom, I love you."
–*Author Unknown*

Mother's and Father's Influence

The Little Parable For Mothers

The young Mother set her foot on the path of life. "Is the way long?" she asked. And her guide said, "Yes. And the way is hard. And you will be old before you reach the end of it. But the end will be better than the beginning."

But the young Mother was happy, and would not believe that anything could be better than these years. So she played with her children, and gathered flowers for them along the way, and bathed them in clear streams, and the sun shone on them and life was good and the young Mother cried, "Nothing will ever be lovelier than this."

Then came night, and storm, and the path was dark, and the children shook with fear and cold, and the Mother drew them close and covered them with her mantle, and the children said, "Oh, Mother, we are not afraid for you are near and no harm can come." And the mother said, "This is better than the brightness of day, for *I have taught my children courage. Today, I have given them strength.*" And the next day came strange clouds which darkened the earth–clouds of war and hate and evil, and the children groped and stumbled, and the Mother said, "Look up. Lift your eyes to the light." And the children looked and saw above the clouds an Everlasting Glory, and it guided them and brought them beyond the darkness. And that night, the Mother said. "This is the best day of all, for *I have shown my children God.*"

And the days went on, and the weeks and the months and the years, and the Mother grew old, and she was little and bent. But her children were tall and strong and walked with courage. And when the way was hard, they helped their Mother and when the way was rough, they lifted her, for she was as light as a feather, and at last they came to a hill, and beyond this hill, they could see a shining road and golden gates flung wide.

And the Mother said, "I have reached the end of my journey. And now I know that the end is better than the beginning, for my children can walk alone, and their children after them." And the children said, "You will always walk with us Mother, even when you have gone through the *gates.*"

Mother's and Father's Influence

And they stood and watched her as she went on alone, and the gates closed after her. And they said, "We cannot see her, but she is with us still. A Mother like ours is *more than a memory. She is a Living Presence.*"

–Temple Baily

True Words Well Said

A father, taking his daughter aside, said, "I want to speak to you of your mother. It may be that you have noticed a careworn look upon her face, lately....it is your duty to help chase it away. I want you to get up tomorrow morning and get breakfast, and when your mother comes and begins to express her surprise, go right up to her and kiss her...You can't imagine how it will brighten her dear face. Besides you owe her a kiss or two.

"Away back when you were a little girl, she kissed you when no one else was tempted by your fever tainted breath and swollen face....And through those years of childish sunshine and shadows she was always ready to cure by the magic of a mother's kiss, the little dirty, chubby hands whenever they were injured in those first skirmishes with this rough old world. And then the midnight kiss with which she routed so many bad dreams as she leaned over your restless pillow, have all been on interest these long years....Her face has more wrinkles than yours, far more; and yet if you were sick that face would appear more beautiful than an angel's as it hovered over you, watching every opportunity to minister to your comfort, and every one of these wrinkles would seem to be bright wavelets of sunshine chasing each other over the dear face.

"She will leave you one of these days. These burdens, if not lifted from her shoulders, will break her down. Those rough, hard hands that have done so many... things for you will be crossed upon her lifeless breast. Those neglected lips that gave you your first baby kiss will be forever closed, and those sad, tired eyes will have opened in eternity, and then you will appreciate your mother, but it will be too late."

–Hearthstone

Mother's and Father's Influence

How We Kept Mother's Birthday

I think celebrating "Mother's Day" once a year is a very good idea..

So we decided to have a special celebration of Mother's Day. We though it a fine idea. We knew how much Mother did for us and so we decided that we should do everything we could to make Mother happy.

We decided to decorate the house with flowers. We asked mother to arrange the decoration because she always does it on holidays. My sisters got new hats for such an important day. We wanted one for Mother too, but she said that she liked her old hat better and didn't want a new one.

Well, after breakfast we decided to take Mother for a beautiful drive away into the country. Mother is never able to go to the country because she is busy in the house nearly all the time.

But then we changed the plan a little. Father decided to take Mother fishing. And when everything was ready for the trip we asked Mother to prepare some sandwiches.

Well, when the car came to the door we saw that there was not enough room in it for us all. Father said that he could stay at home and work in the garden. Then the two girls, Anne and Mary, said that they could stay at home, but as they had new hats, it would be a pity if no one looked at them. In the end it was decided that mother could stay at home and make dinner. Mother doesn't like fishing.

So we all drove away, and Mother stood and watched us from the verandah as long as she could see us.

Well, we had a very nice day in the country. Father caught a lot of big fish and the girls met some friends and they talked about hats. It was quite late when we got back.

At last everything was ready and we sat down to a wonderful dinner. Mother got up and down many times during dinner; she brought things from the kitchen and carried the dishes away.

When the dinner was over all of us wanted to help Mother to wash the dishes. But Mother said that she could do it herself, and so we let her because we wanted to make her happy..

It was quite late when it was all over, and when we all kissed Mother before going to bed, she said it had been the most wonderful day in her life.

–Stephen B. Leaycock

Mother's and Father's Influence

When You Thought I Wasn't Looking

When you thought I wasn't looking I saw you hang my first painting on the refrigerator, and I immediately wanted to paint another one.
When you thought I wasn't looking I saw you feed a stray cat, and I learned that it was good to be kind to animals.
When you thought I wasn't looking, I saw you make my favorite cake for me and I learned that little things can be the special things of life.
When you thought I wasn't looking, I heard you say a prayer, and I knew there is a God I could always talk to and I learned to trust in God.
When you thought I wasn't looking, I saw you make a meal and take it to a friend who was sick, and I learned that we all have to help take care of each other.
When you thought I wasn't looking, I saw you give of your time and money to help people who had nothing, and I learned that those who have something should give to those who don't.
When you thought I wasn't looking, I felt you kiss me good night, and felt loved and safe.
When you thought I wasn't looking, I saw how you handled your responsibilities, even when you didn't feel good, and I learned that I would have to be responsible when I grow up.
When you thought I wasn't looking, I saw tears come from your eyes and I learned that sometimes things hurt, but it's all right to cry.
When you thought I wasn't looking, I saw that you cared, and I wanted to be everything that I could be.
When you thought I wasn't looking, I learned most of life's lessons that I need to know to be a good and productive person when I grow up.
When you thought I wasn't looking, I looked at you and wanted to say, "Thanks for all the things I saw."

—Author unknown

Mother's and Father's Influence

A Dad's Great Job

I may never be as clever
   as my neighbor down the street.
I may never be as wealthy
   as some other men I meet
I may never have the glory
   that some other men have had.
But I've got to be successful
   as a little fellow's dad.

There are certain dreams I cherish
   that I'd like to see come true.
There are things I would accomplish
   ere my working time is through.
But the task my heart is set on
   is to guide a little lad.
And make myself successful
   as that little fellow's dad .

It's the one job that I dream of
   It's the task I think of most.
If I fail that growing youngster
   I'd have nothing else to boast.
I may never come to glory
   I may never gather gold;
Men may count me as a failure
   when my business life is told,

But if he who follows after
   shall be manly, I'll be glad--
For I'll know I've been successful
   as a little fellow's Dad.
For though wealth and fame I'd gather,
   all my future would be sad,
If I failed to be successful
   as that little fellow's Dad.
      –*Author Unknown*

Mother's and Father's Influence

That Boy

He wants to be like his dad!   You men.
Did you ever think, as you pause,
That the boy who watches your every move
Is building a set of laws?

He's molding a life you're the model for,
And whether it's good or bad.
Depends upon the kind of example set
To the boy who'd be like his dad.

Would you have him go everywhere you go?
Have him do just the things you do?
And see everything that your eyes behold,
And woo all the Gods you woo?

When you see the worship that shines in his eyes
Of the lovable little lad,
Could you rest content if he gets his wish?
And grows to be like his dad.

It's a job that none but yourself can fill.
It's a charge you must answer for,
It's a duty to show him the road to tread,
Ere he reaches his manhood's door.

It's a debt you owe for the greatest joy
On this earth to be had;
The pleasure of having a boy to raise
Who wants to be like his dad.

–Author Unknown

Mother's and Father's Influence

To My Grown-up Son

My hands were busy through the day
I didn't have much time to play
The little games you asked me to
I didn't have much time for you.

    I'd wash your clothes, I'd sew and cook,
    But when you'd bring your picture book
    And ask me please to share your fun,
    I'd say: "A little later son."

        I'd tuck you in all safe at night
        And hear your prayers, turn out the light,
        Then tiptoe softly to the door. . .
        I wish I'd stayed a minute more.

    For life is short, the years rush past. . .
    A little boy grows up so fast.
    No longer is he at your side,
    His precious secrets to confide.

The picture books are put away.
There are no longer games to play,
No good-night kiss, no prayers to hear. . .
That all belongs to yesteryear.

        My hands, once busy, now are still,
        The days are long and hard to fill.
        I wish I could go back and do
        The little things you asked me to.
                —*Author Unknown*

Mother's and Father's Influence

Father's Footsteps

A father and his tiny son
Crossed a rough street one stormy day.
"See papa," said the little lad,
"I stepped in your steps all the way."

Ah, random childish hands that deal
Quick thrusts no coat of steel could stay;
It touched him with the touch of steel:
"I stepped in your steps all the way."

If this man shirks his manhood's due,
And heeds what lying voices say,
It is not one that fails, but two,
"I stepped in your steps all the way."

But they who thrust off greed and fear,
Who love and watch, who toil and pray;
How their hearts carol when they hear,
"I stepped in your steps all the way."
—Author unknown

One father is worth more than a hundred school masters.
—George Herbert

Mother's and Father's Influence

What Makes A Dad?

God took the strength of a mountain,
The majesty of a tree,
The warmth of a summer sun,
The calm of a quiet sea,
The generous soul of nature,
The comforting arm of night,
The wisdom of the ages,
The power of the eagle's flight.
The joy of a morning in spring,
The faith of a mustard seed,
The patience of eternity,
The depth of a family need,
Then God combined these qualities,
And then there was nothing more to add,
He knew His masterpiece was complete,
And so, He called it-- *Dad*.
—*Author unknown*

Why God Made Fathers

God knew that children all would need
Someone secure and strong
To shelter and protect them,
And to teach them right from wrong.
Someone to take pride in,
And look up to as a guide,
Someone they could count on,
And in whom they could confide...
He knew as children grew up,
They'd need the reassurance of
Someone with faith and trust in them,
Who would always give them love...
And that's why God made Fathers.
—*Author Unknown*

Mother's and Father's Influence

Only A Dad

Only a dad with a tired face,
Coming home from the daily race,
Bringing little of gold or fame
To show how well he has played the game,
But glad in his heart that his own rejoice
To see him come home and to hear his voice.

Only a dad with a brood of four,
One of ten million or more
Plodding along in the daily strife,
Bearing the whips and the scorns of life,
With never a whimper of pain or hate,
For the sake of those who at home await.

Only a dad, neither rich nor proud,
Merely one of the surging crowd,
Toiling, striving from day to day,
Facing whatever may come his way,
Silent whenever the harsh condemn,
And bearing it all for the love of them.

Only a dad, but he gives his all
To smooth the way for his children small,
Doing with courage stern and grim
The deeds that his father did for him.
This is the line that for him I pen;
Only a dad, but the best of men.

–Edgar A. Guest

Mother's and Father's Influence

Dad

These memories are of our dad
   Who's always been just swell–
He's helped us out so often
   Has been a pal as well.
He worked for us and planned for us
   Has shown us good times too,
And he has tried to show his love
   By all the things he'd do.

Our dad is not like other guys
   He's someone set apart,
To know the hopes and plans
   In all his children's hearts.
He's someone you can talk to
   When things aren't going right;
He's always there to help you
   When life don't seem so bright.
He may not be the wisest man
   That we shall ever see
But what dad knows about living
   Is good enough for me.

God, bless our dad
   And give us gratitude to see
How much of all his time and thought
   Were given to us free.
Keep courage in his loving heart;
   Direct his useful brain;
Uphold his strength, increase his joys,
   And heal all fear and pain.
Keep us near to all the best,
   And let our father see
That through his constant care and love
   Our lives shall richer be.
      –*Naomi Johnstone*

Mother's and Father's Influence

Man's Greatest Duty

We've never seen the Father here, but we have known the Son,
The finest type of manhood since the world was first begun.
And, summing up the works of God, I write with reverent pen,
The greatest is the Son He sent to cheer the lives of men.

Through Him we learned the ways of God and found the Father's love;
The Son it was who won us back to Him who reigns above.
The Lord did not come down himself to prove to men His worth,
He sought our worship through the Child He placed upon the earth.

How can I best express my life? Wherein does greatness lie?
How can I long remembrance win, since I am born to die?
Both fame and gold are selfish things; their charms may quickly flee,
But I'm the father of a boy who came to speak for me.

In him lies all I hope to be; his splendor shall be mine;
I shall have done man's greatest work if only he is fine.
If some day he shall help the world long after I am dead
In all that men shall say of him my praises shall be said.

It matters not what I may win of fleeting gold or fame,
My hope of joy depends alone on what my boy shall claim.
My story must be told through him; for him I work and plan,
Man's greatest duty is to be the father of a man.

–Edgar A. Guest

Mother's and Father's Influence

"Please Daddy Let's Go"

A little girl with shining eyes, her little face aglow, Said,

"Daddy, it's almost time for Sunday School, please let's go.
They teach us there of Jesus' love, of how he died for all
Those who on Him will call."

"Oh, No!" said Daddy, "not today. I've worked hard all the week,
And I must have one day of rest, I'm going to the creek.
For there I can relax and rest, and fishing's fine, they say.
So run along; don't bother me, we'll go to church someday."

Months and years have passed away, but daddy hears that
plea no more;
"Let's go to Sunday School." Those childish days are o'er.
And, now that daddy's growing old, when life is almost through,
He finds some time to go to church but what does daughter do?

She say's "Oh, daddy, not today– I stayed up almost all night
And I've got to get some sleep, Besides I look a fright!"
Then daddy lifts a trembling hand to brush away the tears,
As again he hears the pleading voice, distinctly through the years.
He sees a small girl's shining face upturned with eyes aglow.
As she says, "It's time for Sunday School,
Please daddy, won't you go?"

    –Author Unknown

Mother's and Father's Influence

Fathers And Sons

Last evening, about five o' clock, four brethren were riding down Main Street. Just as they passed First South Street, they heard a plaintive little cry, "Papa! papa! Wait!" The father was driving, and his ready ear recognized his son's voice. He brought the auto instantly to a standstill. As the men looked out they saw coming out of that bustling, crowd of humanity, a little nine-year old boy, out of breath, panting, crying because of his effort to get to his father, to overtake the auto which he had spied going along Main Street.

The father said, "Why, where have you been, my son? I have been looking for you. Did you leave the place where it was appointed to meet?"

"Yes, I went up to see where you were."

The child understood that he was to meet in front of the tabernacle. The father evidently meant to meet the child farther down the street. However, the son had become separated from his parents, and the little child was thrown into that vast throng, unprotected because of the misunderstanding.

Is there a misunderstanding between you and your sons? Is there one wandering amidst the throngs of life, surrounded by all kinds of temptations? Are you expecting to meet him at an appointed place which he does not know? If so, he may not come out from that throng and cry, "Father, Father." If he should your ears might be deaf to that call, because of the concentration of your mind upon the affairs of life. So you might speed by him and leave him in the midst of evil, to find his way home.

Take your sons with you along this road of life, that you may have them with you in that eternal home where there is everlasting peace and contentment.

–Author Unknown

Mother's and Father's Influence

My Father's Hands

His hands were rough and exceedingly strong. He could gently prune a fruit tree or firmly ease a stubborn horse into a harness. What I remember most is the special warmth from those hands as he would take me by the shoulder and point out the glittering swoop of a blue hawk, or a rabbit asleep in its lair. They were good hands that served him well and failed him in only one thing. They never learned to write.

My father was illiterate. The number of illiterates in our country has steadily declined, but if there were only one I would be saddened, remembering my father and the pain he endured because his hands never learned to write. He started school in the first grade, where the remedy for a wrong answer was ten ruler strokes across a stretched palm. For some reason, shapes, figures and letters just did not fall into the right pattern inside his six year old mind. His father took him out of school after several months and set him to a man's job on the farm.

Years later, his wife, with her fourth-grade education, would try to teach him to read. And still later I would grasp his big fist between my small hands and awkwardly help him to trace the letters of his name. He submitted to the ordeal for a short time, but soon grew restless and would declare that he had had enough.

One night, when he thought no one saw he slipped away with my second grade reader and labored over the words until they became too difficult. He pressed his forehead into the pages and wept. Thereafter, no amount of persuading could bring him to sit with pen and paper. He did still like to listen to my mother, and then to me, read to him. He especially enjoyed listening to us read to him from the Bible.

My father was forced to let the bank take possession of most of the acreage of his farmland one year when a crop failure meant he couldn't make the mortgage payment. He was able to keep one acre of the farmland where the small frame house was located.

From the farm to road building and later to factory work, his hands served him well. His mind was keen, and his will to work was unsurpassed. His enthusiasm and efficiency brought an offer to become a line boss–until he was handed the qualification test.

Mother's and Father's Influence

Years later, when Mother died, I tried to get him to come and live with my family, but he insisted on staying in the small house with the garden plot and a few farm animals close by. His health began to fail, and he was in and out of the hospital with two mild heart attacks.

Old Doc Green saw him weekly and gave him medication, including nitroglycerin tablets to put under his tongue should he feel an attack coming on.

My last fond memory of Dad was watching as he walked across the brow of a hillside meadow with those big warm hands resting on the shoulders of my two children. He stopped to point out a pond where he and I had fished years before. That night, my family and I flew back to our own home. Three weeks later Dad was dead because of a heart attack.

I returned to my father's home for the funeral. Doc Green told me how sorry he was. In fact, he was bothered a bit, because he had just written Dad a new prescription, and the druggist had filled it. Yet the bottle of pills had not been found on Dad's person. Doc Green felt that a pill might have kept him alive long enough to summon help.

I went out to Dad's garden plot where a neighbor had found him. In grief, I stooped to trace my fingers in the earth where he had reached the end of his life. My hand came to rest on a half-buried brick, which I aimlessly lifted. I noticed underneath it the twisted and batted, yet unbroken, container that had been beaten into the soft earth..

As I held the container of pills, the scene of Dad struggling to remove the cap and in desperation trying to break it with the brick flashed painfully before my eyes. With deep anguish I knew why those big hands had lost in their struggle with death. For there, imprinted on the cap, were the words: "child-proof–cap, push down and twist to unlock" The druggist later confirmed that he had just started using the new safety caps.

I knew it was not a rational act, but I went right downtown and bought a leather-bound pocket dictionary and a gold pen set. I bade Dad good-bye by placing them in those big hands once so warm, which had lived so well, but had never learned to write.

–Account by Calvin R. Worthington

Mother's and Father's Influence

His Example

There are little eyes upon you, and they're watching night and day;
There are little ears that quickly take in every word you say;
There are little hands all eager to do everything you do,
And a little boy that's dreaming of the day he'll be like you.

You're the little fellow's idol, you're the wisest of the wise;
In his little mind about you no suspicions ever rise;
He believes in you devoutly, holds that all you say and do
He will say and do in your way when he's grown up just like you.

Oh, it sometimes makes me shudder when I hear my boy repeat
Some careless phrase I've uttered in the language of the street;
And it sets my heart to grieving when some little fault I see
And I know beyond all doubting that he picked it up from me.

There's a wide-eyed little fellow who believes you're always right,
And his ears are always open and he watches day and night;
You are setting an example every day in all you do
For the little boy who's waiting to grow up to be like you.

–Edgar A. Guest

If the Best in boys were found in more men;
The Best in men would be found in more boys.
–Author Unknown

Mother's and Father's Influence

A Father's Prayer

Build me a son, O Lord, who will be strong enough to know when he is weak, and brave enough to face himself when he is afraid; one who will be proud and unbending in honest defeat, and humble and gentle in victory...

Lead him...not in the path of ease and comfort...but let him learn to stand up in the storm...let him learn compassion for those who fail.

Build me a son whose heart will be clear, whose goal will be high...a son who will master himself before he seeks to master other men; one who will learn to laugh, yet never forget how to weep; one who will reach into the future, hut never forget the past.

After all these things are his, add, I pray, enough of a sense of humor, so that he may always be serious, yet never take himself too seriously.
Give him humility, so that he may remember the simplicity of true greatness, the open mind of true wisdom, the meekness of true strength.

Then I, his father will dare to whisper, *"I have not lived in vain."*
                                          –Author Unknown

You ask me to name the best mother of all,
Why really I thought that you knew.
The question is easy, no trouble at all,
I think you can answer it too.

If we were to name two mothers,
On this wonderful day; most noble and fine.
The question is simple, just answer and say;
Our mother; your mother and mine.
       –Author Unknown

Mother's and Father's Influence

The Making Of A Lasting Marriage

The making of a lasting marriage begins with being the right person and prayerfully selecting the right companion.
It must begin with total commitment having a firm foundation of common values, goals and objectives.
It is maintaining an atmosphere of harmony and peace.
It is understanding the little every-day things as well as big things that divide or cement a lasting relationship.
It is developing tolerance for diversity of opinions while striving to reach agreeable solutions.
It is establishing an atmosphere of sincere praise and thoughtful appreciation of even the smallest acts of loving kindness and passing along a warm smile or wiping away a tear.
It is being a builder not a destroyer by creating a wholesome atmosphere in which to grow.
It is encouraging and helping each other develop ones talents and to reach ones potentials.
It is being a good listener and being sensitive to criticism which chips away at each others character and destroys ones *self-respect* and *self-worth*.
It is remembering to express these magic words,
"Thank You" "Please" "I Love You."
It is never ending a single day with unresolved anger or doubts.
It is showing forth the ability to *forget and forgive* when misjudged or treated wrongfully.
It is remembering to *begin* and *end* each day on bended knee with loved ones to express sincere gratitude to our *Creator*, for ones' family and for the many blessings of each day.–*LWH*

You can't pull while you are kicking, you can't kick while you are pulling.

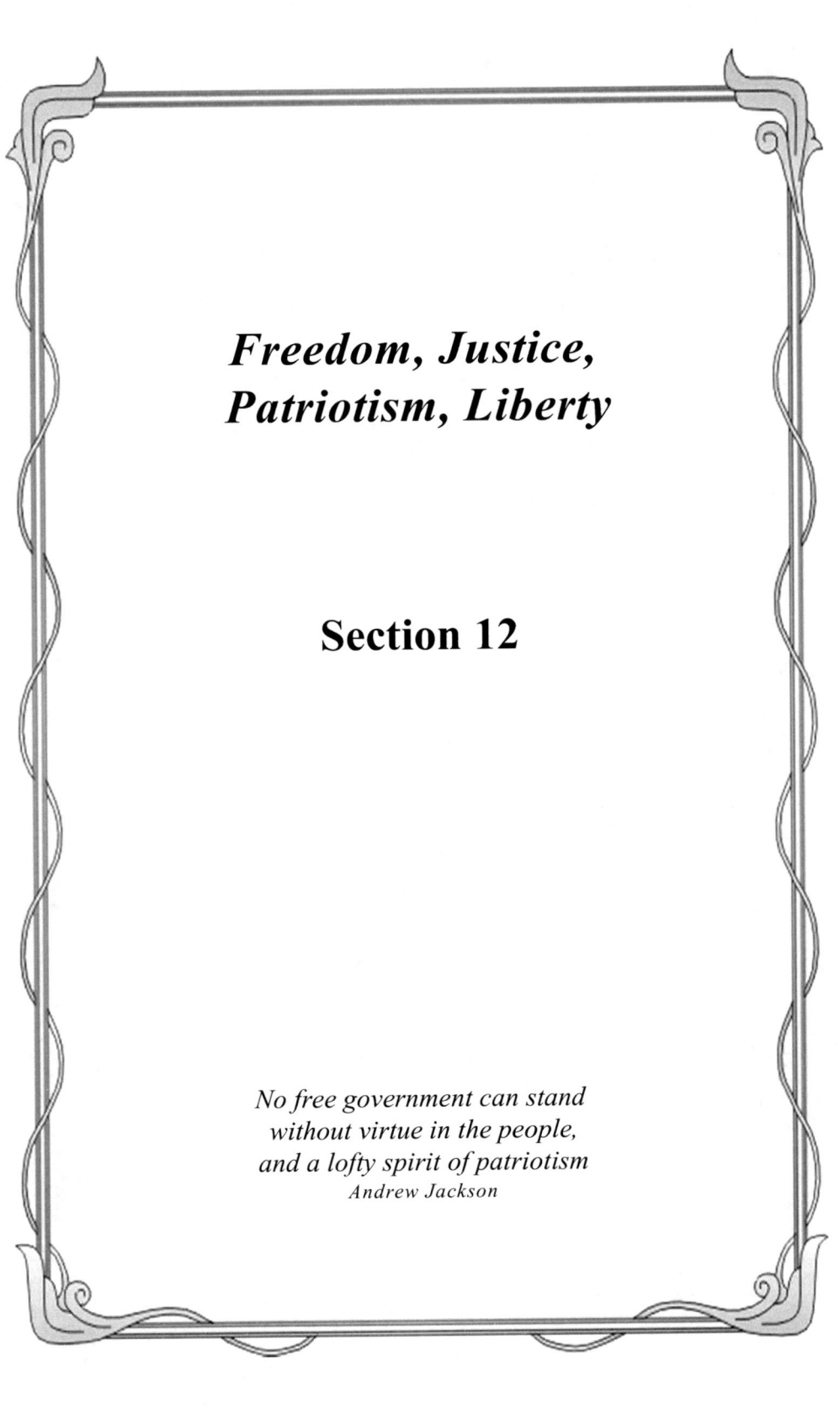

Freedom, Justice, Patriotism, Liberty

Section 12

*No free government can stand
without virtue in the people,
and a lofty spirit of patriotism*
Andrew Jackson

Freedom, Justice, Liberty, Patriotism

Is life so dear, or peace so sweet, as to be purchased at the price of chains and slavery? Forbid it, Almighty God! I know not what course others may take; but as for me, give me liberty or give me death! —*Patrick Henry*

If men be good, government cannot be bad.
—*William Penn*

What is liberty without wisdom and without virtue?
—*Edmund Burke*

There is no liberty to men who know not how to govern themselves.
—*Henry Ward Beecher*

No free government can stand without virtue in the people, and a lofty spirit of Patriotism. . . Thank God my life has been spent in a land of liberty. —*Andrew Jackson*

Labour to keep alive in your breast that little spark of a celestial fire,-- **conscience**.
—*George Washington*

The best thing about the future is that it comes only one day at a time. —*Abraham Lincoln*

Ideas are not limited to territorial borders; they are the common inheritance of all free people.
—*Franklin D. Roosevelt*

Who then is free? The wise man who can govern himself.
—*Horace*

The test of our progress is not whether we add more to the abundance of those who have much; it is whether we provide enough for those who have too little.
—*Franklin D. Roosevelt*

We must all hang together, or assuredly we shall all hang separately.
—*Benjamin Franklin (At the signing of the Declaration of Independence, 5 July, 1775)*

Those who deny freedom to others deserve it not for themselves.
—*Abraham Lincoln*

Freedom, Justice, Liberty, Patriotism

True patriotism is a matter of deeds, not words; of unselfish acts, not hero dreams; of devoted service, not merely sentiment.
–Sir Walter Scott

A house divided against itself cannot stand. I believe this government cannot endure permanently half slave and half free. I do not expect the Union to be dissolved- - I do not expect the house to fall- -but I do expect it will cease to be divided. It will become all one thing, or all the other.
–Abraham Lincoln

Let every nation know, whether it wishes us well or ill, that we shall pay the price, bear any burden, meet any hardship, support any friend, oppose any foe to assure the survival and the success of liberty.
–John F. Kennedy

There are two freedoms–the false, where a man is free to do what he likes; the true, where he is free to do what he ought.
–Charles Kingsley

America is great because America is good, and if America ever ceases to be good, America will cease to be great.
–Alexis de Tocqueville

This is a world of compensation; and he who would be no slave must consent to have no slave. Those who deny freedom to others deserve it not for themselves, and, under a just God, cannot long retain it.
–Abraham Lincoln

Remember always that all of us. . . Are descendants from immigrants and revolutionists.
–Franklin D. Roosevelt

There are two good things in life, Freedom of thought and Freedom of action.
–William Sommerset Maughan

No man can suffer too much, and no man can fall too soon, if he suffer, or if he fall , in the defense of the liberties and constitution of his country.
–Daniel Webster

Freedom, Justice, Liberty, Patriotism

If we work upon marble, it will perish; if on brass, time will efface it; if we rear temples, they will crumple into dust; but if we work upon immortal minds, and imbue them with principles, with the just fear of God and love of our fellow men, we engrave on those tablets something that will brighten to all eternity.
 —*Daniel Webster*

In his life he was a great American. He is an American no longer. He is one of those figures of whom there are few in history, who lose their nationality in death. They are no longer Greek or Hebrew, English or American; they belong to the common people of every land. They love that haggard face with the sad and tender eyes. There is worship in their regard. There is faith and hope in that worship. —*Lloyd George, (unvailing of Lincoln Statue; Westminister, England)*

Men must be governed by God or they will be ruled by tyrants.
 —*William Penn*

Know this that every soul is free,
To choose his life and what he'll be.
For this eternal truth is given,
That God will force no man to heaven.

He'll call, persuade, direct aright,
Bless with wisdom, love and light.
In nameless ways be good and kind,
But never force the human mind.

Freedom and reason make us men,
Take these away, what are we then?
Mere animals, and just as well,
The beasts may think of heaven or hell. —*William C. Clegg*

Give me your tired, your poor,
Your huddled masses yearning to
 breathe free;
The wretched refuse of your
 teeming shore.
Send these, the homeless,
 tempest-tossed to me,
I lift my lamp beside the golden
 door. —*Emma Lazarus*

Freedom, Justice, Liberty, Patriotism

A democracy, -- that is a government of all the people, by all the people, for all the people, Of course, a government of the principles of eternal justice, the unchanging law of God, for shortness' sake I will call it the idea of Freedom.
—*Theodore Parker*

The fate of the country...does not depend on what kind of paper you drop into the ballot box once a year, but on what kind of man you drop from your chamber into the street every morning.
—*Henry David Thoreau*

They are slaves who fear to speak
For the fallen and the weak...
They are slaves who dare not be
In the right with two or three.
—*James Russell Lowell*

PATRIOTISM consists not in waving the flag, but in striving that our country shall be righteous as well as strong.
—*James Bryce*

Almighty God, we make our earnest prayer that Thou wilt keep the United States in Thy holy protection; that Thou wilt incline the hearts of the citizens to cultivate a spirit of subordination and obedience to government; to entertain a brotherly affection and love for one another and for their fellow citizens...
—*George Washington*

I believe in the United States of America as a Government of the people, by the people, for the people; whose just powers are derived from the consent of the governed; a democracy in a republic, a sovereign Nation of many sovereign States; a perfect Union one and inseparable; established upon those principles of freedom, equality, justice and humanity for which American patriots sacrificed their lives and fortunes. I therefore believe it is my duty to my country to love it, to support its Constitution to obey its laws, to respect its flag, and to defend it against all enemies.
The American's *creed*
—*William. T. Page*

Freedom, Justice, Liberty, Patriotism

We have been the recipients of the choicest bounties of heaven. We have grown in numbers, wealth and power as no other nation has ever grown. But we have forgotten God. We have vainly imagined in the deceitfulness of our hearts that all these blessings were produced by success; we have become too self-sufficient to feel the necessity of redeeming grace, too proud to pray to that God who made us. It behooves us then to humble ourselves before the offended Power, to confess our national sins and to pray for clemency and forgiveness.

–Abraham Lincoln

Breathes there the man with soul so dead,
Who never to himself hath said:
"This is my own, My native land!"
Whose heart hath ne'er within him burned,
As home his footsteps he hath turned,
From wandering on a foreign strand?
If such there breaths, go, mark him well;
For him no minstrel raptures swell;
High though his titles, proud his name,
Boundless his wealth, as wish can claim;
Despite those titles, power and pelf,
The wretch, concentered all in self,
Living, shall forfeit fair renown,
And, doubly dying, shall go down
To the vile dust from whence he sprung,
Unwept, unhonored, and unsung.
    –Sir Walter Scott in "Lay of the Last Minstrel"

Freedom, Justice, Liberty, Patriotism

The Makers Of The Flag

This morning, as I passed into the Land Office, the Flag dropped me a most cordial salutation, and from its rippling folds I heard it say: "Good Morning, Mr. Flag Maker."

"I beg your pardon, Old Glory," I said, "Aren't you mistaken? I am not the President of the United States, nor a member of Congress, nor even a general in the army. I am only a Government clerk."

"I greet you again, Mr. Flag Maker," replied the voice. "I know you well. You are the man who worked in the swelter of yesterday straightening out the tangle of that farmer's homestead in Idaho, or perhaps you found the mistake in that Indian contract in Oklahoma, or helped clear that patent for the hopeful inventor in New York, or pushed the opening of that new ditch in Colorado, or made that mine in Illinois more safe, or brought relief to the old soldier in Wyoming. No matter; whichever one these beneficent individuals you may happen to be, I give you greeting, Mr. Flag Maker."

I was about to pass on, when The Flag stopped me with these words;

"Yesterday the President spoke a word that made happier the future of ten million peons in Mexico; but that act looms no larger on the flag than the struggle which the boy in Georgia is making to win the Corn Club prize this summer.

"Yesterday the Congress spoke a word which will open the door of Alaska; but a mother in Michigan worked from sunrise until far into the night, to give her boy an education. She, too, is making the flag.

"Yesterday we made a new law to prevent financial panics, and yesterday, maybe, a school teacher in Ohio taught his first letters to a boy who will one day write a song that will give cheer to the millions of our race. We are all making the flag."

"But," I said impatiently, "these people were only working!"

Then came a great shout from the Flag:

"The work that we do is the making of the flag.

"I am not the flag; not at all. I am but its shadow. I am whatever you make me, nothing more.

Freedom, Justice, Liberty, Patriotism

"I am your belief in yourself, your dream of what a people may become.

"I live a changing life, a life of moods and passions, of heartbreaks and tired muscles.

"Sometimes I am strong with pride, when men do an honest work, fitting the rails together truly.

"Sometimes I droop, for then purpose has gone from me, and cynically I play the coward.

"Sometimes I am loud, garish, and full of that ego that blasts judgment.

"But always, I am all that you hope to be, and have the courage to try for.

"I am song and fear, struggle and panic, and ennobling hope.

"I am the day's work of the weakest man, and the largest dream of the most daring.

"I am the Constitution and the courts, statutes and the statute makers, soldier and dread-naught, drayman and street sweep, cook, counselor, and clerk.

"I am the battle of yesterday, and the mistake of tomorrow.

"I am the mystery of the men who do without knowing why.

"I am the clutch of an idea, and the reasoned purpose of resolution.

"I am no more than what you believe me to be and I am all that you believe I can be.

"I am what you make me, nothing more.,

"I swing before your eyes as a bright gleam of color, a symbol of yourself, the pictured suggestion of that big thing which makes this nation. *My stars and my stripes are your dreams and your labors..* They are bright with cheer, brilliant with courage, firm with faith, because you have made them so out of your hearts. For you are the makers of the flag and it is well that you glory in the making."

–Frank K. Lane (1937)

Freedom, Justice, Liberty, Patriotism

With malice toward none; with Charity for all; with firmness in the right, as God gives us to see the right, let us strive on to finish the work we are in; to bind up the nation's wounds; to care for him who shall have borne the battle and for his widow, and his orphan—to do all which may achieve and cherish a just and lasting peace among ourselves and with all nations.
–*Abraham Lincoln (Mar. 4, 1865, 2nd Inaugural address)*

God who gave us life gave us liberty. Can the liberties of a nation be secure when we have removed a conviction that these liberties are the gift of God? Indeed I tremble for my country when I reflect that God is just, that his justice cannot sleep forever.
–*Thomas Jefferson*

If we and our posterity shall be true to the Christian religion, if we and if they shall live always in the fear of God and shall respect His commandments, if we and they shall maintain just moral sentiments, we may have the highest hopes of the future fortunes of our country, and we may be sure of one thing: Our country will go on prospering. But if we and our posterity reject religious instruction and authority, violate the rules of eternal justice, trifle with the injunctions of morality, and recklessly destroy the political Constitution which holds us together, no one can tell how sudden a catastrophe may overwhelm us, that shall bury all our glory in profound obscurity.
–*Daniel Webster*

Freedom, Justice, Liberty, Patriotism

The Responsive Chord

In the early spring of 1863, when the Confederate and Federal armies were confronting each other on the opposite hills of Stafford and Spottsylvania, two bands chanced one evening, at the same hour, to begin to play sweet music on either bank of the river. A large crowd of the soldiers of both armies gathered to listen to the music. Soon the bands began to answer each other. First the band on the northern bank would play "*Star Spangled Banner*," "*Hail Columbia*," or some other National air, and at the conclusion the "boys in blue" would cheer most lustily, and then the band on the southern bank would respond with "*Dixie*" or "*Bonnie Blue Flag*," or some other Southern melody, and the "boys in gray" would attest their approbation with an old "Confederate yell." But presently one of the bands struck up, in sweet and plaintive notes, which were wafted across the beautiful Rappahannock, were caught up at once by the other band and swelled into a grand anthem which touched every heart, "*Home Sweet Home*."

At the conclusion of this piece there went up a simultaneous shout from both sides of the river–cheer followed cheer, and those hills, which had so recently resounded with hostile guns, echoed and re-echoed the glad acclaim..

A chord had been struck responsive to which the hearts of enemies—enemies that could beat in unison; and, on both sides of the river, Something down the soldiers' cheeks washed off the stains of powder.

–*J. William Jones*

Freedom, Justice, Liberty, Patriotism

A Beautiful Allegory

An eminent Kentucky lawyer, once used the following allegory in defense of a poor feeble minded person:

"When God conceived the plan of creating man he called the three angels that waited on His throne, **Justice, Truth and Mercy**, and said, 'Shall we make man?'

"***Justice*** said, 'Make him not, O God, he will trample upon thy laws.'

Truth also answered, 'Make him not, O God, he will pollute your sanctuaries.'

Mercy kneeling and looking up through her tears, said, 'Make him, O God, and I will watch over him in the dark hours of his life.'

"So God made man and said, '*O Man, thou art the **child of Mercy***; go out and live with thy brother." *(Portland, (Me.) Transcript, 1851.)*

Dear Madam:

I have been shown in the files of the War Department a statement of the Adjutant-General of Massachusetts that you are the mother of five sons who have died gloriously on the field of battle. I feel how weak and fruitless must be any words of mine which should attempt to beguile you from the grief of a loss so overwhelming. But I cannot refrain from tendering to you the consolation that may be found in the thanks of the Republic they died to save. I pray that our heavenly Father may assuage the anguish of your bereavement, and leave you only the cherished memory of the loved and lost, and the solemn pride that must be yours to have laid so costly a sacrifice upon the altar of freedom.

–*Abraham Lincoln, (A letter to Mrs. Bixby, Nov 21, 1864.)*

Freedom, Justice, Liberty, Patriotism

Faith, Hope And Charity

Patriotism isn't marching behind a band and puffing out your chest. Patriotism isn't a flash of fireworks one day of the year, and the submerging one's emotions the rest of the year. Patriotism isn't found in the whooping of the crowd or maudlin flag-waving.

Patriotism is the sum of the three cardinal virtues: Faith, Hope, and Charity. *Faith* in the principles of our government; *Hope* in the future of our country; *Charity* toward all and malice toward none.

Patriotism is that spirit that makes us help our neighbors when they are in distress, and extend sympathy when they are striken.

Patriotism is the tugging at our heart-strings, and sincere kinship with those who toil in field or shop or marketplace.

Patriotism is the emotion that makes a lump rise in the throat when some intrepid spirit strives to achieve something that no human being ever before achieved.

Patriotism is to be unashamed at the moisture that comes welling up in our tear ducts with the passing of some great and noble soul, who unselfishly devoted his life to the cause of mankind.

Patriotism is loving one's country, respecting its traditions and honoring its people, whether high or low, rich or poor.

Patriotism is standing firm and unselfish for the right, for the common good, for the peace and well-being of all; sacrificing self, if need be, and unafraid against all opposition. *–New England Adage*

The Bible is the source of liberty. I have always said and always will say that the studious perusal of this Sacred Volume will make better citizens.
–Thomas Jefferson

True patriotism is a matter of deeds, not words; of unselfish acts, not hero dreams; of devoted service, not mere sentiment.
–Sherwood Eddy

Freedom, Justice, Liberty, Patriotism

So it's home again, and home again,
America for me!
My heart is turning home again
And there I long to be
Oh London is a man's town power in the air;
And Paris is a woman's town, with flowers in her hair
I want a ship that's westward bound
to plough the rolling sea,
To the blessed land of room enough
Beyond the ocean bars,
There the air is full of sunlight and
The flag is full of stars.
–Henry Van Dyke

Once to every man and nation comes the moment to decide,
In the strife of Truth with Falsehood for the good or evil side.
–James Russell Lowell

Freedom, Justice, Liberty, Patriotism

Oh Captain! My Captain!

(Written in memory of President Lincoln, to whom the poem refers
 as the captain of the ship of State.)

Oh Captain! My Captain! Our fearful trip is done,
The ship has weathered every rack, the prize we sought is won.
The port is near, the bells I hear, the people all exulting,
While follow eyes the steady keel, the vessel grim and daring:
      But O heart! Heart! Heart!
       O the bleeding drops of red,
         Where on the deck my Captain lies,
        Fallen cold and dead.

O Captain! my Captain! Rise up and hear the bells;
Rise up—for you the flag is flung—for you the bugle trills,
For you bouquets and ribbon'd wreaths–for you the shores
   a-crowding.
For you they call, the swaying mass, their eager faces turning;
      Hear Captain! dear father!
       This arm beneath your head!
        It is some dream that on the deck,
         You've fallen cold and dead.

My Captain does not answer me, his lips are pale and still,
Mr father does not feel my arm, he has no pulse nor will,
The ship is anchored safe and sound, its voyage closed and done,
From fearful trip the victor ship comes in with objective won;
      Exult, O shores, and ring O bells!
       But I with mournful tread,
        Walk the deck; my Captain lies
         Fallen cold and dead.
          –*Walt Whitman*

What were you carrying, Pilgrims, Pilgrims?
What did you carry beyond the sea?
   We carried the Book, we carried the Sword,
   A steadfast heart in the fear of the Lord,
   And a living faith in His plighted word
That all men should be free.
–Francis Brett Young

To The Boys of America

Of course what we have a right to expect from the American boy is that he shall turn out to be a good American man. Now, the chances are strong that he won't be much of an man unless he is a good deal of a boy. He must not be a coward or a weakling, a bully, a shirk or a prig. He must work hard and play hard. He must be clean-minded and clean-lived, and able to hold his own under all circumstances and against all comers. It is only on these conditions that he will grow into the kind of a man of whom America can really be proud. In life, as in a football game, the principle to follow is: Hit the line hard; don't foul and don't shirk, but hit the line hard.
–Theodore Roosevelt

When it shall be said in any country in the world, "My poor are happy; neither ignorance nor distress is to be found among them; my jails are empty of prisoners, my streets of beggars; the aged are not in want, the taxes are not oppressive; the rational world is my friend, because I am a friend of its happiness"-when these things can be said, then may that country boast of its constitution and its government.
–Thomas Paine

Happiness, Friendship, Kindness

Section 13

*Blessed are the peacemakers
For they shall be called
The children of God.*
Matthew 5:9

Happiness, Friendship, Kindness

People are lonely because they build walls instead of bridges.
—*Joseph F. Newton*

When angry, count ten before you speak, if very angry, count a hundred.
—*Thomas Jefferson*

Kindness is like fresh-fallen snow; it makes beautiful everything that it covers.
—*Author Unknown*

If you treat a man as he is, he will remain as he is, but if you treat him as if he were what he ought to be, and could be, he will become what he ought to be, and should be.
—*Goethe*

I never did anything worth doing by accident, nor did any of my inventions come by accident. They came by work.
—*Thomas A. Edison*

The greatest gifts you'll ever give though with them never part, Are simply these: a helping hand, And a selfless, loving heart.
—*Author Unknown*

The grand essentials of happiness are: Something to do, Something to love, And something to hope for.
—*Author Unknown*

Life is not so short but there is always time enough for courtesy.
—*Ralph Waldo Emerson*

Blessed are they who have the gift of making friends, for it is one of God's best gifts. It involves many things, but above all, the power of going out of one's self, and appreciating whatever is noble and loving in another.
—*Thomas Hughes*

Happiness, Friendship, Kindness

Assuredly all nature informs us that man is born for happiness.
—Andre Gide

A man that hath friends must show himself friendly.
—Author Unknown

Don't expect to enjoy the cream of life if you keep your milk of human kindness all bottled up.
—Author Unknown

When a person is down in the world, an ounce of help is better than a pound of preaching.
—Bulwer Lytoon

Friendship consists of forgetting what one gives and remembering what one receives.
—Author Unknown

It is necessary to the happiness of man that he be mentally faithful to himself.
—Thomas Paine

Kindness

I have wept in the night
For the shortness of sight
That to somebody's need
Made me blind;
But I never have yet
Felt a tinge of regret
For being a little too kind.
—Author unknown

You give but little when you give of your possessions. It is when you give of yourself that you truly give.
—Kahlil Gibran

One of the most tragic things I know about human nature is that all of us tend to put off living. We are all dreaming of some magical rose garden over the horizon instead of enjoying the roses that are blooming outside our windows today.
—Dale Carnegie

Success is getting what you want; Happiness is wanting what you get.
—Dale Carnegie

Happiness, Friendship, Kindness

Much happiness is overlooked because it doesn't cost anything.
—*Author Unknown*

We are as happy as we make up our minds to be.
—*Abraham Lincoln*

The secret of happiness is not in doing what one likes to do, but in liking what one has to do.
—*Sir James M. Barrie*

If all men were to bring their miseries together in one place, most would be glad to take each his own home again rather than take a portion out of the common stock. —*Solon*

We cannot tell the precise moment when friendship is formed. As in filling a vessel drop by drop, there is at last a drop which makes it run over; so in a series of kindnesses there is at last one which makes the heart run over.
—*Samuel Johnson*

Happiness is like jam--you can't spread even a little without getting some on yourself.
—*Author Unknown*

A slender acquaintance with the world must convince every man that actions, not words, are the true criteria of the attachment of friends; and that the most liberal professions of good will are very far from being the surest marks of it.
—*George Washington*

Kindness is one thing you can't give away. It always comes back.
—*Sidney Skolsky*

A friend is one who knows all about you and loves you just the same.
—*Author Unknown*

Don't ever take a fence down until you know the reason why it was put up
—*Gilbert Keith Chesterton*

Happiness, Friendship, Kindness

Happiness adds and multiplies as we divide it with others.
—*Ralph Waldo Emerson*

The finest kind of friendship is between people who expect a great deal of each other but never ask it.
—*Author Unknown*

Some people come into our lives and quickly go. Some stay awhile and leave footprints on our hearts, and we are never ever the same.
—*Author Unknown*

Kindness is produced by kindness.
—*Cicero*

A friend is a jewel that shines brightest in the darkness of misfortune.
—*Author Unknown*

If we lose affection and kindness from our life, we lose all that gives it charm.
—*Cicero*

My Friend
It is my joy in life to find
At every turning of the road,
The outstretched arm of Comradship
To help me onward with my load.
But tho' I have no gold to give,
And love alone must make amends;
My only hope is while I live,
God make me worthy of my friends.
—*Author Unknown*

What wealth it is to have such friends that we cannot think of them without elevation.
—*Henry David Thoreau*

The best part of a good man's life is his little, nameless, unremembered acts of kindness and love.
—*William Wordsworth*

His daily prayer, far better understood in acts than in words, was simply doing good.
—*John Greenleaf Whittier*

Happiness, Friendship, Kindness

The Arrow And The Song

I shot an arrow into the air,
It fell to the earth, I knew not where;
For, so swiftly it flew, the sight
Could not follow it in flight.

I breathed a song into the air,
It fell to the earth, I knew not where;
For who had sight so keen and strong,
That it can follow the flight of song?

Long, long afterward, in an oak
I found the arrow , still unbroke;
And the song, from beginning to end,
I found again in the heart of a friend.
  –Henry Wadsworth Longfellow

A friend is a present you give yourself.
  –Robert Louis Stevenson

Growing Friendship

Friendship is like a garden
of flowers, fine and rare,
It cannot reach perfection
except through loving care;
Then, new and lovely blossoms
with each new day appear....
For friendship, Like a garden,
grows in beauty year by year
  –Anna Holden King

Happiness, Friendship, Kindness

Friendship is love without its wings.
—*Byron*

A Friend

Of all the treasures one can find
Until his life has reached its end,
There really isn't anything
Of greater value than a friend.

> A friend is all you'll ever need
> When times of crisis are at hand
> And you are looking all about
> For someone who will understand.

And when a sadness fills your heart
And only darkness you can see,
It helps a lot to have a friend
Who at your side right then can be.

> Or if you feel a loneliness
> That simply will not go away,
> It's wonderful to have a friend
> To bring you smiles across the day.

I know it would be hard for me
Without a loyal friend or two;
Especially the kind of friend
That I have always found in you.
—*Author Unknown*

Happiness, Friendship, Kindness

One never knows
How far a word of kindness goes;
One never sees
How far a smile of friendship flees.
Down, through the years,
The deed forgotten reappears.

One kindly word
The souls of many here has stirred.
Man goes his way
And tells with every passing day,
Until life's end:
"Once unto me he played his friends."

We cannot say
What lips are praising us today.
We cannot tell
Whose prayers ask God to guard us well.
But kindness lives
Beyond the memory of him who gives.
–Author Unknown

With kindness you can give a man back his self-respect,
You can bring life to smothered dreams,
You can mend broken hearts,
You can bring heaven down to earth.
–Author Unknown

Happiness, Friendship, Kindness

A Friend

A friend is a person or something
 That likes you, who knows,
 It may be a child or a kitten,
A grownup, a bird or a rose.

Tree friends will give you shadows
 And a lovely place to swing;
 Or crooked limbs for climbing,
Or blossoms to smell in the spring.

A breeze is a friend, and a lake is,
 It invites you to cool your toes;
 And a little wind will fan you,
 And carry a scent to your nose.

So you never need to be lonely,
 Just look for a simple clue.
There is always something or someone
 Who wants to be a friend to you.
 –*Author Unknown*

Happiness consists more in small conveniences
 or pleasures that occur every day,
Than in great pieces of good fortune that happen
 but seldom to a man in the course of his life.
 –*Benjamin Franklin*

Happiness, Friendship, Kindness

Touching shoulders

There's a comforting thought at the close of the day
When I'm weary and lonely and sad,
That sort of grips hold of my crusty old heart
And bids it merry and glad.
It gets in my soul and drives out the blues,
And finally thrills through and through;
It is just a sweet memory that chants the refrain
I'm glad I touched shoulders with you!

Did you know you were brave,
Did you know you were strong?
Did you know there was one leaning hard?
Did you know that I waited and listened and prayed,
And was cheered by your simplest word?
Did you know that I longed for that smile on your face,
For the sound of your voice ringing true?
Did you know I grew stronger and better because
I had merely touched shoulders with you?

I am glad that I live, that I battle and strive
For the place that I know I must fill;
I am thankful for sorrows; I'll meet with a grin
What fortune may send, good or ill.
I may not have wealth, and I may not be great,
But I know I shall always be true,
For I have in my life that courage you gave
When once I rubbed shoulders with you.
—*Author Unknown*

A friend is someone you can be alone with and have nothing to do
and not be able to think of anything to say
and be comfortable in the silence.
—*Sheryl Condie*

Happiness, Friendship, Kindness

Important Words

The five most important words are -
"I am proud of you"
The four most important words are -
"What is your opinion?"
The two most important words are -
"Thank you"
The least important word is -
"I"
–Author Unknown

I Meant To Do My Work Today

I meant to do my work today–
But a brown bird sang in the apple tree,
And a butterfly flitted across the field,
And all the leaves were calling me.

And the wind went sighing over the land,
Tossing the grasses to and fro,
And a rainbow held out its shining hand-
So what could I do but laugh and go.
–Richard Le Gallienne

Happiness, Friendship, Kindness

Good-Bye

There is a word, of grief the sounding token;
There is a word bejeweled with bright tears,
The saddest word fond lips have ever spoken;
A little word that breaks the chain of years;
Its utterance must ever bring emotion,
The memories it crystals cannot die,
`Tis known in every land, on every ocean--
`Tis called "Goody-bye."[7]
*(Said to have been written in a friend's album,
by Ah Foo Lin,.)*

Crossing Paths With You

When the even'in shades are falling
at the closing of the day.
And we're just a sit'in around
passing the time away,
There's a thought that's going to cheer us,
when we're feeling kind of blue,
Just a little prayer of gratitude for
crossing paths with you.

So we're giving you this message
just because we want to say,
That we're glad God arranged it
so that we might pass your way.
Just to see you and to know you
made our sky a shade more blue,
And we're just a bit more happy
since crossing paths with you.
–*Author Unknown*

Happiness, Friendship, Kindness

Around The Corner

Around the corner I have a friend,
In this great city that has no end;
Yet days go by and weeks rush on,
And before I know it a year is gone,
And I never see my old friend's face;
For life is a swift and terrible race.
He knows I like him just as well,
As in days when I rang his bell
And he rang mine. We were young then;
And now we are busy, tired men--

Tired with playing a foolish game;
Tired with trying to make a name.
"Tomorrow", I say, "I will call on Jim,
Just to show that I'm thinking of him."
But tomorrow comes--and tomorrow goes;
And the distance between us grows and grows.
Around the corner!--yet miles away--
"Here's a telegram, Sir" --"Jim died today".
And that's what we get--and deserve in the end,
Around the corner, a vanished friend.
—Charles Hanson Towne

Don't walk in front of me, I may not follow.
Don't walk behind me, I may not lead.
Just walk beside me, and be my friend.
—Author Unknown

Happiness, Friendship, Kindness

Ten Rules For Happiness

1. Develop yourself by self-discipline.
2. Joy comes through creation--sorrow through destruction. Every living thing can grow; use the world wisely to realize soul growth.
3. Do things which are hard to do.
4. Entertain up-building thoughts. What you think about when you do not have to think shows what you really are.
5. Do your best this hour and you will do better the next.
6. Be true to those who trust you.
7. Pray for those things such as wisdom, courage, and a kind heart.
8. Give heed to God's message through inspiration. If self-indulgence, jealousy, avarice or worry have deadened your response, pray to the Lord to wipe out these impediments.
9. True friends enrich life. If you would have friends, be one.
10. Faith is the foundation of all things, including happiness.

–David O. McKay

Look Up!

Look up! and not down;
Out! and not in;
Forward and not back;
And lend a hand.
(Edward Everett Hale's Motto
for The Lend-a-Hand Society)
–Author Unknown

Happiness does not come from doing easy work but from the afterglow of satisfaction that comes after the achievement of a difficult task that demanded our best efforts.

–Author Unknown

Happiness, Friendship, Kindness

Good-Morning

Good morning, Brother Sunshine;
  Good-morning, Sister Song.
I beg your humble pardon
  If you've waited very long.
I thought I heard you rapping;
  To shut you out were sin.
My heart is standing open;
  Won't you walk right in?

Good-morning, Brother Kindness;
  Good-morning, Sister Cheer.
I heard you were out calling,
  So I waited for you here.
Some way I keep forgetting
  I have to toil and spin
When you are my companions;
  Won't you walk right in?
    – J.W. Foley

Goodness

A good deed is never lost.
He who sows courtesy, reaps friendship;
He who plants kindness gathers love;
Pleasure bestowed upon a grateful mind was never sterile,
Generally gratitude begets reward.
    –Basil

Happiness, Friendship, Kindness

Requisites For Contented Living

Health enough to make work a pleasure;

Wealth enough to support your needs;

Strength enough to battle with difficulties and to forsake them

Grace enough to confess your sins and overcome them;

Charity enough to see some good in your neighbor;

Love enough to move you to be useful and helpful to others;

Faith enough to make real the things of God;

Hope enough to remove all anxious fears concerning the future.
—*Goethe*

Kindness is a language which the deaf can hear and the blind can read.
—*Mark Twain*

Die when I may, I want it said of me by those who knew me best, that I always plucked a thistle and planted a flower where I thought a flower would grow. —*Abraham Lincoln*

Do not keep the alabaster boxes of your love and tenderness sealed up until your friends are dead. Fill their lives with sweetness. Speak approving, cheering words while their ears can hear them and while their hearts can be thrilled by them. —*Henry Ward Beecher*

Happiness, Friendship, Kindness

There never was a day that did not bring its own opportunity for doing good, that never could have been done before, and never can be again.
–W.H. Burleigh

He who wants to do a great deal of good at once will never do anything. Life is made up of little things. It is very rarely that an occasion is offered for doing a great deal at once. True greatness consist in being great in little things –C. Simmons

A Simple Prayer

Lord, make me an instrument of Thy peace.
Where there is hatred, let me sow love,
Where there is injury, pardon,
Where there is darkness, light,
Where there is sadness, joy,
Where there is doubt, faith,
And where there is despair, hope.

O Divine Master,
Grant that I may not so much seek
To be consoled as to console,
To be understood as to understand,
To be loved as to love.
For it is in giving that we receive
It is in forgiving that we are pardoned,
And it is in dying that we are born to Eternal Life.
–St. Francis-Assisi

Happiness, Friendship, Kindness

Happiness itself is sufficient excuse. Beautiful things are right and true; so beautiful actions are those pleasing to the gods. Wise men have an inward sense of what is beautiful, and the highest wisdom is to trust this intuition and be guided by it. The answer to the last appeal of what is right lies within a man's own breast. Trust thyself
—Aristotle

Can You Say

Can you say in parting with the day
that's slipping fast,
That you helped a single person of the
many you have passed?
Is a single life rejoicing over what you
did you said?
Does someone whose hopes were fading,
now with courage look ahead?

Did you waste the day or lose it,
was it well or poorly spent?
Did you leave a trend of kindness,
or a scar of discontent?
As you close your eyes in slumber,
do you think that God would say—
You have made the world much better
for the life you've lived today?
—Author Unknown

Happiness, Friendship, Kindness

In exact proportion as you give joy you will receive joy. It is a law of exact reciprocity. Joy increases as you give it, and diminishes as you try to keep it for yourself. Actually, unless you give it you will ultimately lose it. In giving it you will accumulate a deposit of joy greater than you ever believed possible.

–Author Unknown

Silent Friendship

That friendship runs too deep for speech
The most of us know well.
The heart can feel but not reveal
What oft it aches to tell.

Twix tongue and heart a chasm lies
Which speech can seldom cross
Who would impart what's in the heart
For words seem at a loss.

Too deep for phrase devotion runs
Too deep for tongue or pen
Genius alone can quite make known
Its thoughts to other men.

And so in silence for the most
Our years are lived away,
And friends must guess
What deeds express
But lips can never say.

–Author Unknown

Happiness, Friendship, Kindness

A Favorite Recipe

Take a cup of *Kindness*
Mix it well with *Love*...
Add a lot of *Patience*
And *Faith* in God above...
Sprinkle very generously
With *Joy* and *Thanks* and *Cheer*...
And you'll have lots of
"Angel Food"
To feast on all the year!
–Author Unknown

The Heart Of Friendship

Here's to the heart of friendship, tried and true,
That laughs with us when joys our pathway strew;
And kneels with us when sorrow, like a pall,
Enshrouds our stricken souls; then smiles through all
The midnight gloom with more than human faith.
Here's to the love that seeks not self, and hath
No censure for our frailty, but doth woo,
By gentle arts, our spirits back into
The way of truth; then sheds upon our lives
A radiance that all things else survives.
–Author Unknown

He who has a thousand friends
has not a friend to spare,
And he who has one enemy
shall meet him everywhere.
–Ali Ben Abu Taleb

Happiness, Friendship, Kindness

A Friend

If I could find a friend today,
I would not ask for greater store;
If just one soul would come and say,
"We shall be comrades evermore,"

I would not need to count my gold
Tonight, when busy labors end–
My heart a greater wealth would hold,
If I could say, "I made a friend."

If I today a friend could find,
Amid the labor and the stress,
Some toiling brother, kindred mind,
Some hand to clasp in tenderness,

It would not matter what reward
The hours had brought me on the way–
If I could say, "I thank Thee, Lord,
I know I made a friend today.
 –*Author Unknown*

When one door of happiness closes, another opens;
but often we look so long at the closed door
that we do not see the one which has been opened for use.
 –*Helen Keller*

Happiness, Friendship, Kindness

The Two Seekers

Two men went seeking happiness—
One walked the roadside way
And looked with all his longing eyes
Within each garden along the way.
Where'er he saw it growing
He tried to grasp its flower;
But always in his clutching hand,
It died before an hour;
Till, angry and despairingly
In bitterness he cried,
"Others are given happiness,
To me it is denied."

The other one looked around him—
Since happiness is found
In other people's gardens,
Why not within my grounds?"
He dug and plowed and planted,
And with a careful toil
Where it was rough and stony,
Enriched each inch of soil,
Until with crowded blossoms
The little plot o'erran—
"How simple 'tis," the owner cried,
"To be a happy man!"
–*Priscilla Leonard*

Happiness, Friendship, Kindness

They planted a seed in my heart that day,
   And it grew from that tiny thing
   'Til it filled my heart with new desire
   And gave my soul a truer ring.

   My only thought was of work undone
     Timely tasks so hard to do.
   When the mind is tired, 'tis a tragic thing,
     It seems one never gets through.

But they came to my door with a smile for me
   A hand clasp of love and cheer,
And I rested a bit as we talked that day
   'Til my mind began to clear.

   They brought me a message that lifted me up,
     Gave me courage to face that day
   Gave me hope and strength to go on again
     But in a different way.

Did they know, they had given all that to me?
   Can they know the good they do?
The souls they lift, the hearts they cheer,
   The seeds they planted that grew!

   May they have God's blessings with them always
     As each day they do their part.
   May He ever be near them with those gifts
     They give to that other heart.
        –*Author Unknown*

Happiness, Friendship, Kindness

The King And The Shirt

One day the king became very ill. He called his wise men to gather around him to help decide how he could be cured. "I will give half my kingdom to the man who can cure me," he said to his wise men. No one seemed to have any suggestions for the king, except one of the wise men. He stepped forward and said, "If you can find a happy man in the kingdom, take his shirt, put it on the king–and the king will be cured."

Immediately the king sent his messengers to search for a happy man. They traveled for days, far and wide over the entire kingdom. They could not find a man who was completely satisfied. If he was rich, he was ailing. If he was healthy, he was poor. If he was both rich and healthy, he had a cross wife. If he had children they were unruly. It appeared that everyone in the kingdom had something to complain of.

Finally, as the king's son was returning to the castle late one evening, he passed by a poor little hut. As he stopped, he heard someone say, "Now, God be praised, I have finished my work, I have eaten my fill, and I can lie down and sleep! What more could I possibly want? Nothing!"

The king's son was sure that this was the man they had been searching for. He immediately gave orders that the man's shirt be seized and carried to the king. The man was to be given as much money as he wanted.

The messenger quick to obey entered the little hut to take off the man's shirt, but the happy man was so poor that he had no shirt.

— *A fable by Leo Tolstoy, written about a hundred years ago.*

Happiness, Friendship, Kindness

The Praying Hands

In a small chapel at Northwestern University, there is a statue of a pair of gnarled but devoutly folded hands raised in prayer. The story behind this five- hundred year old masterpiece of art – has a strange story of an amazingly sacrificial friendship.

This story from France goes back to the year 1490 where two very talented young apprentices Franz Knigstein and Albrecht Durer struggled to support themselves so they could studied art. Working took much of their time. Often they confided in one another their desire to study painting in some of the great cities of Europe. Because they were poor such studies would take a lot of money.

Finally they had a solution. They would draw lots, and one of them would work to support both of them while the other studied. . Albrecht won and he went to Venice to study. They agreed that when Albrecht was successful, he would support Franz who would then study art. Franz worked at hard labor as a black-smith to support them both. As quickly as he received his wages, he would forward them to his friend.

The months stretched into years, and at last Albrecht returned to his native land an independent master. As the world now knows, he had not only talent but genius. He had attained success and went back to keep his bargain with Franz. The two met in joyous reunion, but when Albrecht looked at his friend, tears welled from his eyes. He soon discovered the enormous price his friend had paid. For as Franz worked at hard manual

Happiness, Friendship, Kindness

labor to support them, his gnarled fingers had become stiff and twisted. His slender, sensitive hands had been ruined for life. Franz's fingers could never execute the delicate brush strokes necessary for fine painting. Though Fran's artistic dreams were shattered, he was not embittered, but rather rejoiced in his friend's success.

One day Albrecht came upon Franz unexpectedly, and found him kneeling with his gnarled hands intertwined in prayer, quietly praying for the success of his friend although, he himself could no longer be an artist. Albrecht, the great genius, in humble gratitude, hurriedly sketched the folded hands of his faithful friend and later completed a truly great masterpiece known as "The Praying Hands." Albrecht presented his painting to his devoted friend, Franz, who had labored so that he himself might develop his talent.

Today, art galleries everywhere feature Albrecht Durer's works. But of them all, none holds the place in the hearts of people that "The Praying Hands" does. It tells an eloquent story of friendship, love, sacrifice, labor and gratitude. That is why the masterpiece was reproduced in the chapel at Northwestern.

–An adaptation of the story by J. Palmer Muntz's

Happiness, Friendship, Kindness

The Old Fisherman

Our house was directly across from the clinic entrance of John Hopkins Hospital in Baltimore. We lived downstairs and rented the upstairs rooms to outpatients at the clinic. One summer evening as I was fixing supper, there was a knock at the door. I opened it to see a truly awful looking old man.

"Why he's hardly taller than my eight-year-old," I thought as I stared at the stooped, shriveled body. But the appalling thing was his face--lopsided from swelling, red and raw. Yet his voice was pleasant as he said, "Good evening, I've come to see if you've a room for just one night. I came for a treatment this morning from the seashore, and there's no bus till morning."

He told me he'd been hunting for a room since noon but with no success. "I guess it's my face. I know it looks terrible, but my doctor says with a few more treatments..."

For a moment I hesitated but his next words convinced me, "I could sleep in this rocking chair on the porch. My bus leaves early in the morning."

I told him we would find him a bed, but to rest on the porch meanwhile. Then I went inside and finished getting supper. When we were ready, I asked the old man if he would join us. "No thank you. I have plenty." And he held up a brown paper bag.

When I had finished the dishes, I went out on the porch to talk with him a few minutes. It didn't take long to see that this old man had an over-sized heart crowded into that tiny body. He told me that he fished for a living to support his daughter, her five children, and her husband, who was hopelessly crippled from a back injury. He didn't tell it by way of complaint; every other sentence was prefaced with a thanks to God for a blessing.

Happiness, Friendship, Kindness

He was grateful that no pain accompanied his disease, which was apparently a form of skin cancer. He thanked God for giving him the strength to keep going.

At bedtime, we put a camp cot in the children's room for him. When I got up in the morning, the bed linens were neatly folded and the little man was out on the porch. He refused breakfast, but just before he left for his bus, haltingly, as if asking a great favor, he said, "Could I please come back and stay the next time I have a treatment? I won't put you out a bit--I can sleep fine in a chair. Your children make me feel at home. Grownups are bothered by my face, but children don't seem to mind."

I told him he was welcome to come again. And on his next trip he arrived a little after seven in the morning. As a gift, he brought a big fish and a quart of the largest oysters I had ever seen. He said he had shucked them that morning before he left so they would be nice and fresh. I knew his bus left at four a.m. and wondered what time he had to get up in order to do this.

In the years he came to stay overnight with us there was never a time that he did not bring us fish or oysters or vegetables from his garden. Other times we received packages in the mail, always by Special Delivery; fish and oysters packed in a box of fresh young spinach or kale, every leaf carefully washed. Knowing that he must walk three miles to mail these and how little money he had, made the gifts doubly precious.

When I received these little remembrances, I often thought of a comment our next-door neighbor made after he left that first morning. "Did you keep that awful looking man last night? I turned him away. You can lose roomers by putting up such people."

And maybe we did once or twice. But, Oh! If only they could have known him, perhaps their illnesses would have been easier to bear. I know our family always will be grateful to have known him; from him we learned what it was to accept the bad without complaint and the good with gratitude to God. Recently I was visiting a friend who has a greenhouse. As she showed me her flowers we came to the most beautiful one of all; a golden chrysanthemum, bursting with blooms. But to my great surprise it was growing in an old, dented, rusted bucket. I thought to myself, if this were my plant I'd put it in the loveliest container I had. My friend changed my mind.

"I ran short of pots," she explained, "and knowing how beautiful this one would be, I thought it wouldn't mind starting out in this old pail. It's just for a little while, till I can put it out in the garden."

She must have wondered why I laughed so delightedly, but I was imagining just such a scene in heaven. "Here's an especially beautiful one," God might have said when he came to the soul of the fisherman. "He won't mind starting in this small body."

But that's behind now, long ago, and in God's garden how tall this lovely soul must stand.

–Author Unknown

Happiness, Friendship, Kindness

Drop A Pebble In The Water

Drop a pebble in the water: just a splash, and it is gone;
But there's half-a-hundred ripples circling on and on and on,
Spreading, spreading from the center, flowing on out to the sea.
And there is no way of telling where the end is going to be.

Drop a pebble in the water: in a minute you forget,
But there's little waves a-flowing, and there's ripples circling yet,
And those little waves a-flowing to a great big wave have grown;
You've disturbed a mighty river just by dropping in a stone.

Drop an unkind word, or careless: in a minute it is gone;
But there's half-a-hundred ripples circling on and on and on.
They keep spreading, spreading, spreading from the center as they go,
And there is no way to stop them, once you've started them to flow.

Drop an unkind word, or careless: in a minute you forget;
But there's little waves a-flowing and there's ripples circling yet,
And perhaps in some sad heart a mighty wave of tears you've stirred,
And disturbed a life was happy, ere you dropped that unkind word.

Drop a word of cheer and kindness: just a flash and it is gone;
But there's half-a-hundred ripples circling on and on and on,
Bearing hope and joy and comfort on each splashing, dashing wave
Till you wouldn't believe the volume of the one kind word you gave.

Drop a word of cheer and kindness: in a minute you forget;
But there's gladness still a-swelling and there's joy circling yet,
And you've rolled a wave of comfort whose sweet music can be heard
Over miles and miles of water just by dropping one kind word.

– James W. Foley

Happiness, Friendship, Kindness

A Rose A Twig And A Lily

In ancient Japan, there was a scholar who went out of the gates and came in at nights and gave a lecture to the workmen whom he met. One day as he started out to get his lessons from nature, a man approached him and said, "Will you please bring me tonight a rose that I may see the lessons you mentioned last evening?"

"Yes, I will bring you a rose."

A second one accosted him and said, "Will you bring a twig such as you used to illustrate your lecture last evening?"

"Yes I will bring you a twig."

And a third, "Will you bring me a lily that I may study the lesson of purity you gave?"

And he promised to bring the lily. At sundown, after work, the three laborers were there to meet the educator, philosopher. To the first he gave the rose to the second the twig, and to the third the lily.

Suddenly the one with the rose said, "Why, here is a thorn clinging to the stem of my rose."

The second said, "And here is a dead leaf on my twig."

Encouraged by the remarks, the third man said, "And here is dirt clinging to the roots of my lily."

"Let me see." And the educator took from the first the rose, from the second the twig, and from the third the lily. From the rose he plucked the thorn, and keeping the flower, handed the thorn to the first. He took the dead leaf from the twig and gave it to the second, took the dirt from the roots of the lily and handed it to the third.

"There," he said, "each of you has what attracted him first. You looked for the thorn and found it. I left it there. I left the dead leaf and you saw that first. You have it. You saw the dirt clinging to the roots of your lily, and I have placed that in your hand. I will keep the rose, the twig, and the lily, for the beauty I see in them."

–Author unknown

Happiness, Friendship, Kindness

In each one of us there may be a dead leaf clinging to our reputation, or a thorn in our character, there may even be a little dirt. We should ask ourselves "what are we looking for?" Surely one will find a rose, or a lily or a twig if one looks for the best in others or ourselves. (Matt. 7:2) "For with what judgement ye judge, ye shall be judged, and with what measure ye meet it shall be measured to you again."   *L.W.H.*

We can complain because roses have thorns
Or be glad because thorns have roses.
    –Author Unknown

Lincoln And The Birds

One of the most interesting incidents of which I have ever read or heard is connected with the memory of one of the greatest and noblest men of all times--Abraham Lincoln.

In company with some other candidates who were out on a political campaign over a half century ago in the wild West, he saw in the woods near the close of the day some baby birds that had been blown out of their nest. Asking to be allowed to get down from the carriage, which passed on ahead, Mr. Lincoln picked up the tiny creatures and restored them to their little home.

On reaching the inn, he was asked the cause of his delay, and astonished his hearers by telling them of his human act, declaring that, had he not returned the birdies to their mother's care, he could not sleep at night. What a tender loving heart.

    –Author Unknown

Happiness, Friendship, Kindness

The House By The Side Of The Road

"He was a friend to man, and lived
in a house by the side of the road."
—Homer

There are hermit souls that live withdrawn
In the peace of their self-content;
There are souls, like stars, that dwell apart,
In a fellowless firmament:
There are pioneer souls that blaze their paths
Where the highways never ran;
But let me live in a house by the side of the road
And be a friend to man.

Let me live in a house by the side of the road,
Where the race of men go by–
The men who are good, and the men who are bad,
As good and as bad as I.
I would not sit in the scorner's seat,
Or hurl the cynic's ban;
Let me live in a house by the side of the road
And be a friend to man.

Happiness, Friendship, Kindness

I see from my house by the side of the road,
By the side of the highway of life,
The men who press with the ardor of hope,
The men who are faint with the strife.
But I turn not away from their smiles nor their tears–
Both parts of an infinite plan;
Let me live in my house by the side of the road
And be a friend to man.

I know there are brook-gladdened meadows ahead,
And mountains of wearisome height;
That the road passes on through the long afternoon,
And stretches away to the night.
But still I rejoice when the travelers rejoice,
And weep with the strangers that moan,
Nor live in my house by the side of the road
Like a man who dwells alone.

Let me live in my house by the side of the road,
Where the race of men go by–
They are good, they are bad, they are weak,
they are strong,
Wise, foolish--so am I.
Then why should I sit in the scorner's seat,
Or hurl the cynic's ban?–
Let me live in my house by the side of the road
And be a friend to man.

–*Sam Walter Foss*

Crowded Ways Of Life
(Written in reply to The House By The Side Of The Road)

'Tis only a half truth the poet has sung
Of the "house by the side of the way."
Our Master had neither a house nor a home,
But he walked with the crowd day by day.
And I think, when I read of the poet's desire,
That the house by the road would be good;
But service is found in its tenderest form
When we walk with the crowd in the road.

So I say, Let me walk with the men in the road,
Let me seek out the burdens that crush,
Let me speak a kind word of good cheer to the weak
Who are falling behind in the rush.
There are wounds to be healed, there are breaks we must mend,
There's a cup of cold water to give;
And the man in the road by the side of his friend
Is the man who has learned to live.

Then tell me no more of the house by the road;
There is only one place I can live–
It's there with the men who are toiling along,
Who are needing the cheer I can give.
It is pleasant to live in the house by the way
And be a friend, as the poet has said;
But the Master is bidding us: "Bear ye their load,
For your rest waiteth yonder ahead."

Happiness, Friendship, Kindness

I could not remain in the house by the road
And watch as the toilers go on,
Their faces beclouded with pain and with sin,
So burdened their strength nearly gone.
I'll go to their side, I'll speak in good cheer,
I'll help them to carry their load;
And I'll smile at the man in the house by the way,
As I walk with the crowd in the road.

Out there in the road that goes by the house,
Where the poet is singing his song,
I'll walk and I'll work 'midst the heat of the day,
And I'll help falling brothers along–
Too busy to live in the house by the way,
Too happy for such an abode.
And my heart sings its praise to the Master of all,
Who is helping me serve in the road.

–Walter A Gresham

Happiness, Friendship, Kindness

There Are Loyal Hearts

There are loyal hearts, there are spirits brave,
   There are souls that are pure and true;
Then give to the world the best you have,
   And the best shall come back to you.

Give love, and love to your heart will flow,
   A strength in your utmost need;
Have faith, and a score of hearts will show
   Their faith in your word and deed.

For life is the mirror of king and slave,
   'Tis just what you are and do;
Then give to the world the best you have,
   And the best will come back to you.
    –Madeline S. Bridges

Life is short but there is always time for courtesy.
   –Ralph Waldo Emerson

There is no duty we so much underrate as the duty of being happy.
By being happy we sow anonymous benefits upon the world.
   –Robert Lewis Stevenson

Life, Talents, Time, Values

Section 14

*A man who dares to
waste one hour of life
has not discovered the value of life.*
Charles Darwin

Life, Talents, Time, Values

The business of life is to go forward. —Samuel Johnson

An old man living alone, was asked if he wasn't lonely. The answer was: I have a past that's worth living again. No man could ask for more.
—Author Unknown

Life is not complex if you walk straight. —Author Unknown

If the end of life is to enjoy life, then we should so live that enjoyment will be possible to the end.
—Author Unknown

Life has value only when it has something valuable as its object.
—George W. Hegel

The measure of life is not length, but honesty.
—John Lyly

Life is learning, improving, repenting, serving.
—Author Unknown

A good reputation is more valuable than money.
—Author Unknown

Do not put off living today because this is the only time we have.
—Author Unknown

To do two things at once, is to do neither. —Publius Syrus

Life is a grindstone; whether it grinds you down or polishes you up depends on what you are made of.
—Author Unknown

Life is amply long for him who orders it properly. —Seneca

Endeavor to so live that when you die even the undertaker will be sorry. —Mark Twain

Yesterday is a history,
Tomorrow is a mystery,
Today is a gift,
That's why it's called, the present.
—Author Unknown

Life, Talents, Time, Values

Life is not a goblet to be drained; it is a measure to be filled.
—Author Unknown

A sound head, an honest heart, and a humble spirit are the three best guides through time and to eternity.
—Sir Walter Scott

Why is there never enough time to do it right
But always enough time to do it over?
—Author Unknown

Everything comes to him who hustles while he waits.
—Thomas Edison

Do It Now

I expect to pass through this world but once. Any good thing, therefore, that I can do or any kindness I can show to any fellow human being let me do it now. Let me not defer nor neglect it, for I shall not pass this way again.
—Stephen Grellet

Life consists in what man is thinking of all day.
—Ralph Waldo Emerson

I have given you life - now make the most of it.
—Author Unknown

All the world's a stage, and all the men and women merely players; They have their exits and their entrances, And one man in his time plays many parts...
—Shakespeare

What is time? The shadow on the dial, the striking of the clock, the running of the sand,
Time. . . life. . . choice. . .
The very essence of all we are or shall ever be.
—Henry W. Longfellow

The question of life is not, How much time have we?- - - for in each day, each of us has exactly the same amount: We have all there is! The question is: What shall we do with it?
—Anna R. Lindsay

Manana is often the busiest day of the week.
—Spanish Proverb

Life, Talents, Time, Values

Life itself can't bring you joy.
Life can't give you happiness.
No matter how you will it,
It only gives you time and space
It's up to you to fill it.
  –*Author Unknown*

Life is God's gift to you.
What you do with it is your gift to God. –*Author Unknown*

Life is a road of trials and decisions.
The way we prepare to meet these trials and make decisions, determines the Joy and Sorrow of our lives. –*Author Unknown*

Nothing is more unworthy of a wise man, or ought to trouble him more, than to have allowed more time for trifling and useless things than they deserved. –*Plato*

I still find each day too short for all the thought I want to think, all the walks I want to take, all the books I want to read, and all the friends I want to see.
  –*John Burroughs*

The highest of all arts is the art of living well.
Beyond the beauty of sculpture and painting,
Of poetry and music, is the beauty of a well spent life
Here all can be artists, every man a hero. –*Author Unknown*

Many of us look for the time when we'll reach our destination instead of enjoying the journey.
  –*Author Unknown*

It is better to be right and stand alone than to be wrong and have company.
  –*Author Unknown*

Driftwood

It is not the seconds the clock ticks off
Nor the days as they come and go,
That determines our course on the stream of life,
But whether we drift or row.
  –*Author Unknown*

Life, Talents, Time, Values

𝔄 diamond cannot be polished without friction.
A man cannot be perfected without trials.
— *Author Unknown*

𝔇oth thou love life? Then do not squander time, for that is the stuff life is made o –*Benjamin Franklin*

𝔗he supply of time is a daily miracle. Each day twenty-four hours are given to us to do with as we wish. It is the most precious possession we have, so live it daily and take advantage of every opportunity. –*Author Unknown*

𝔗his time, like all times, is a very good one, if we but know what to do with it
— *Ralph Waldo Emerson*

𝔄 man who dares to waste one hour of life has not discovered the value of life. –*Charles Darwin*

𝔐ay you live all the days of your life. –*Jonathan Swift*

Do It Now

ℑf you have hard work to do,
    Do it now.
Today the skies are clear and blue,
Tomorrow clouds may come in view,
Yesterday is not for you;
    Do it now.

If you have a song to sing
    Sing it now.
Let the tones of gladness ring
Clear as song of bird in Spring,
Let every day some music bring;
    Sing it now.

If you have kind words to say
    Say them now.
Tomorrow may not come your way.
Do a kindness while you may,
Loved ones will not always stay;
    Say them now.

If you have a smile to show,
    Show it now.
Make hearts happy, roses grow,
Let the friends around you know
The love you have before they go;
    Show it now.
— *Charles R. Skinner.*

Life, Talents, Time, Values

What the future has in store for you, depends largely upon what you place in store for the future.
—Author unknown

Little Things

Little drops of water,
Little grains of sand,
Make the mighty ocean
And the pleasant land.

Thus the little minutes,
Humble though they be,
Make the mighty ages
Of eternity.

Thus our little errors
Lead the soul away,
From the path of virtue,
Oft in sin to stray.

Little deeds of Kindness,
Little words of Love,
Make our earth an Eden,
Like the heaven above.
—Frances S. Osgood

Yesterday is a cancelled check
Tomorrow is a promissary note
Today is ready cash–spend it wisely.
—Author Unknown

Today is the day to make memories.
Yesterday is too late.
—Author Unknown

Lost

A precious moment set with golden opportunities.
No reward offered, for it is lost forever.
—Author Unknown

As a man thinketh in his heart, so is he.
—Author Unknown

Learn to see in another's calamity
The ills which you should avoid.
—Pubilius

My father early gave me to understand that a sound serviceable body was essential for a happy and productive life.
—Samuel A. Eliot

Is Life Worth Living?

Is life worth living I ask a friend -
Weary of toil and strife.
He answered me thus, it will all depend
On what you demand of life.

> If pleasure is all you would have-Ho,
> Then life isn't worth living at all.
> For you will find at life's great end,
> That pleasure is wormwood and gall.

If gaining riches great is your aim
Tis a selfish game you have played.
For you will find as others have found
That riches will melt away.

> If living the life of sin is your wish,
> You are treading a dangerous path
> For he who is the master of all has
> Said "The wages of sin is death."

But if you are living the best you can
As you tread life's upward road
If you are helping your fellowmen,
And are leading their steps to God.

> If you go with a smile instead of a frown,
> As you work to this great end,
> Of preparing yourself for eternity,
> Then life is worth living my friend.

–Author Unknown

Life, Talents, Time, Values

Know this that every soul is free,
To choose his life and what he'll be,
For this eternal truth is given.
That God will force no man to heaven.

He'll call, persuade, direct aright,
Bless him with wisdom, love and light.
In nameless ways be good and kind,
But never force the human mind.

Freedom and reason make us men,
Take these away, what are we then?
Mere animals, and just as well,
The beasts may think of heaven or hell.

May we know more our pow'rs abuse
But ways of truth and goodness choose
Our God is pleased when we improve
His grace and seek his perfect love
            –Author unknown c. 1805

I Wish

I wish there was some wonderful place
Called the Land of Beginning Again,
Where all the mistakes and all the heart aches
And all our poor selfish grief
Could be dropped like a shabby old coat
And never put on again.
–Author Unknown

Life, Talents, Time, Values

As I sit alone reflecting
On life's trials past and gone,
There is a thought that gives me courage
And the power to go on.

Looking back o'er all its billows
That once brought me great despair,
Now I wonder how all these ripples
Could have caused such pain and care.

At the time they most o'er whelmed me,
Crushed my faith and power to do,
But as time came to my rescue
It completely changed my view.

Every billow that comes rolling on
To toss us on its crest,
It's just natures way of teaching us
How to do our level best.
If we learn each billows lesson
"Tis an aid our lives to guide,
If we pass it by unheeded
We're just drifting with the tide.

So when trials and tribulations
Come and fill our minds with doubts,
They're to teach some needed lesson
We could never learn without.
　　　　　　　–*James Ivin Holt*

Time is a childhood's leaden wings.
It is age's rushing, soundless river.
　　　　　　　–*Walter de la Mare*

Life, Talents, Time, Values

A man's worth is determined by what he accomplishes, not by what he knows.
—*Author Unknown*

The beauty seen is partly in he who sees it.
—*Author Unknown*

Make the most of yourself, for that is all there is to you.
—*Ralph Waldo Emerson*

Life wasn't meant to be lived in a shell.
—*Author Unknown*

Henry David Thoreau, a man of the 20th Century, gives us some direction:

He went to live on the edge of a pond called Walden. His intent was not to escape life but to find it. Having studied man's great thoughts at Harvard, he concluded that his classes taught all the branches, but none of the roots.

He explained: "I went to the woods because I wished to live deliberately, to front only the essential facts of life, and to see if I could not learn what it had to teach, and not, when I came to die, discover that I had not lived."
—*Henry David Thoreau*

Man's mind is like a garden, which may be intelligently cultivated or allowed to run wild but whether cultivated or neglected, it must, and will, bring forth. If no useful seeds are put into it, then an abundance of useless weed seeds will fall therein, and continue to produce their kind.
—*Author Unknown*

Life, Talents, Time, Values

The Touch Of The Master's Hand

Twas battered and scarred, and the auctioneer
Thought it scarcely worth his while,
To waste much time on the old violin,
But held it up with a smile.

"What am I bid, good folks," he cried,
Who'll start the bid for me?
A dollar, a dollar, then two only two?
Two dollars and who'll make it three?

Three dollars, once three dollars twice;
Going for three--but no,"
From the room far back a gray-haired man
Came forward and picked up the bow,

Then wiping the dust from the old violin,
And tightening the loose strings,
He played a melody pure and sweet
As a caroling angel sings.

The music ceased and the auctioneer
With a voice that was quiet and low,
Said, "What am I bid for the old violin?"
And he held it up with the bow.

"A thousand dollars, and who'll make it two?
Two thousand and who'll make it three?
Three thousand once, three thousand twice,
And going and gone, " said he.

The people cheered, but some of them cried.
We do not quite understand.
What changed its worth?
Swift came the reply,
"The touch of the Master's hand."

Life, Talents, Time, Values

And many a man with life out of tune,
And battered and scarred
Is auctioned cheap to the thoughtless crowd.
Much like the old violin.

    A mess of pottage, a glass of wine,
    A game and he travels on.
    He is going, once and going twice,
    He's going and almost gone.

But the Master comes and the foolish crowd
Never can quite understand,
The worth of a soul and the change that's wrought,
    By the touch of the Master's hand.
        –*Author Unknown*

Frowns

If you frown at life as you go your way,
And grumble and growl the livelong day,
You'll find the world is a sorry place,
A gloomy affair like your frowning face.

But sing a song, like a playful lad,
And whistle a tune, like a youngster glad;
You'll find the world will smile at you,
The sun will shine, and the skies be blue.
        –*Author Unknown*

For every minute you are angry
    you lose sixty seconds of happiness.
        –*Ralph Waldo Emerson*

Life, Talents, Time, Values

It is something to be able to paint a particular picture, or to carve a statue, and so to make a few objects beautiful; but it is far more glorious to carve and paint the very atmosphere through which we look–to affect the quality of the day–that is the highest of the arts.
　　　　　　　　　　　　　　　　–*Henry David Thoreau*

Twelve Things To Remember
1. The value of time
2. The value of perseverance
3. The pleasure of working
4. The dignity of simplicity
5. The worth of character
6. The power of kindness
7. The obligation of duty
8. The virtue of patience
9. The wisdom of economy
10. The improvement of talent
11. The joy of originating
12. The influence of example
　　　　　　　–*Author Unknown*

It is a good thing to have money and the things that money can buy, but it is good, too, to check up once in awhile and make sure we haven't lost the things money can't buy.
　　　　　　　–*Author Unknown*

If you want to make an easy job seem mighty hard, just keep putting off doing it.
　　　　　　　–*Author Unknown*

The best thing about the future is that it comes only one day at a time.
　　　　　　　–*Abraham Lincoln*

We are what we believe we are.
　　　　　　　–*Justice Cardozo*

As if you could kill time without injuring eternity.
　　　　　　　–*Henry David Thoreau*

Dost thou love life? Then do not squander time, For that is the stuff life is made of..
　　　　　　　–*Benjamin Franklin*

Lost, yesterday, somewhere between sunrise and sunset, Two Golden Hours, each set with sixty diamond minutes. No reward is offered, for they are gone forever
　　　　　　　–*Horace Mann*

Life, Talents, Time, Values

To men prepared, delay is always hurtful.   –Dante

By and By never comes.   –St.. Augustine

That which is past and gone is irrevocable; wise men have enough to do with things present and to come.
   –Francis Bacon

We live in the present, we dream of the future, but we learn eternal truths from the past.   –Author Unknown

Don't let yesterday use up too much of today.
   –Will Rogers

Use what talents you possess: the woods would be very silent if no birds sang except those that sang best.
   –Henry Van Dyke

To me every hour of the day and night is an unspeakable perfect miracle.
   –Walt Whitman

The whole life of man is but a point of time; let us enjoy it, therefore, while it last and not spend it to no purpose.
   –Plutarch

Our life is frittered away by detail. . . .Simplify, Simplify.
   –Henry David Thoreau

Life, Talents, Time, Values

What Is Life To You?

To the soldier life's a battle
To the teacher life's a school.
Life's a "good thing" for the grafter
It's a failure to the fool.

To the man upon the engine
Life's a long and heavy grade;
It's a gamble to the gambler;
To the merchant it's a trade.

Life's a picture to the artist;
To the rascal life's a fraud;
Life perhaps, is but a burden
To the man beneath the hod.

Life is lovely to the lover;
To the player life's a play;
Life may be a load of trouble
To the man upon the dray.

Life is but a long vacation
To the man who loves his work.
Life's an everlasting effort
To the ones who like to shirk.

To the earnest Christian worker
Life's a story ever new;
Life is what we try to make it,
Brother, *What is life to you?*
   –Author Unknown

Life, Talents, Time, Values

I believe in the supreme worth of the individual and in his right to life, liberty, and the pursuit of happiness.

I believe that every right implies a responsibility; every opportunity, an obligation; every possession, a duty.

I believe that the law was made for man and not man for the law; that government is the servant of the people and not their master.

I believe in the dignity of labor, whether with head or hand; that the world owes every man an opportunity to make a living.

I believe that thrift is essential to well-ordered living and that economy is a prime requisite of a sound financial structure, whether in government, business or personal affairs.

I believe that truth and justice are fundamental to an enduring social order.

I believe in the sacredness of a promise, that a man's word should be as good as his bond; that character -- not wealth or power or position -- is of supreme worth.

I believe that the rendering of useful service is the common duty of mankind and that only in the purifying fire of sacrifice is the dross of selfishness consumed and the greatness of the human soul set free.

I believe in an all-wise and all-loving God, named by whatever name, and that the individual's highest fulfillment, greatest happiness, and widest usefulness are to be found in living in harmony with His will.

I believe that love is the greatest thing in the world; that it alone can overcome hate; that right can and will triumph over might.

–John D. Rockefeller, Jr.

Life, Talents, Time, Values

The Loom Of Time

Man's life is laid in the loom of time
   To a pattern he does not see,
While the weavers work and the shuttles fly
   Till the dawn of eternity.

Some shuttles are filled with silver threads
   And some with threads of gold,
While often but the darker hues
   Are all that they may hold.

But the weaver watches with skillful eye
   Each shuttle fly to and fro,
And sees the pattern so deftly wrought
   As the loom moves sure and slow.

God surely planned the pattern:
   Each thread, the dark and fair,
Is chosen by His master skill
   And placed in the web with care.

He only knows its beauty,
   And guides the shuttles which hold
The threads so unattractive,
   As well as the threads of gold.

Not till each loom is silent,
   And shutters cease to fly,
Shall God reveal the pattern
   And explain the reason why.

The dark threads were as needful
   In the weaver's skillful hand
As the threads of gold and silver
   For the pattern which He planned.
               –*Author Unknown*

Life, Talents, Time, Values

Life's Lesson

Learn to make the most of life,
Lose no happy day,
Time can never bring thee back
Chances swept away.
Leave no tender word unsaid,
Love while life shall last,
The mill will never turn again
With water that has past.
–Author Unknown

The River Time

Oh! A wonderful stream is the River Time,
As it runs through the realm of tears,
With a faultless rhythm, a musical rhyme
And a broader sweep and a surge sublime
As it bends with the ocean of years.....
–Author Unknown

Life is a gift to be used every day,
Not to be smothered and hidden away;
It isn't a thing to be stored in the chest
Where you gather your keepsakes and treasure your best;
It isn't a joy to be sipped now and then
And promptly put back in a dark place again.

Life is a gift that the humblest may boast of
And one that the humblest may make the most of.
Get out and live in each hour of the day,
Wear it and use it as much as you may;
Don't keep it in niches and corners and grooves,
You'll find that in service its beauty improves.
–Edgar A. Guest

Life, Talents, Time, Values

If You Can Sit At Set Of Sun

If you can sit at set of sun
And count the deeds that you have done
And counting find
One self-denying act, one word
That eased the heart of him that heard—
One glance most kind,
Which fell like sunshine where he went,
Then you may count that day well spent.

But if, thru all the livelong day,
You've cheered no heart, by yea or nay,
If through it all,
You've nothing done that you can trace
That brought the sunshine to one face—
No act most small
That helped some soul and nothing cost—
Then count that day as worse than lost.
—*Robert Browning*

To *mean well* is nothing without to *do well*.
—*Plautus*

Let the scroll
Fill as it may as years unroll;
But when again she calls her youth
To serve her in the ranks of Truth,
May she find all one heart, one soul—
At home or on some distant shore—
"All present, or accounted for!
—*Edward E. Hale*

Life, Talents, Time, Values

When I Have Time

When I have time,
so many things I'll do
To make life happier
And much more fair
For those whose lives are crowded
now with care.
I'll help to lift them from their
low despair,   *When I have time.*

When I have time,
the friend I love so well
Shall know no more
these weary toiling days:
I'll lead her feet in pleasant paths always,
And cheer her heart with words
of sweetest praise, *When I have time.*

When you have time!
The friend you hold so dear
May be beyond the reach of your intent;
May never know that you so kindly meant
To fill her life with love and sweet
content,   *When you had time.*

Now is the time! Ah, friend,
no longer wait
To scatter loving smiles and words of cheer
To those around whose lives are now so drear,
They may not meet you in the coming year–
Now is the time!
–Author Unknown

Life, Talents, Time, Values

Today

Upon the threshold of "today" I stand—
It lies before me, fresh from God's own hand,
Without a blemish-mine, for good or ill.
But, if I trust to self, to my weak will,
To keep it spotless, I shall surely fail;
Thy strength and guidance can alone avail.
So now my heart goes out in earnest pleas,
That, for today, Thou wilt abide with me.
—Author Unknown

The Best Things In Life Are Free

When we count our many blessings
It isn't hard to see
That life's most valued treasures
Are the treasures that are free.

For it isn't what we own or buy
That signifies our wealth.
It's the special gifts that have no price;
Our family, friends and health.
—Author Unknown

Don't waste time. Don't waste it in idleness; don't waste it in regretting the time already wasted; don't waste it in dissipation; don't waste it in resolutions a thousand times repeated never to be carried out. Don't waste your time. Use all of it. *Sleep, work, rest, think.*
—Arthur Brisbane

Life, Talents, Time, Values

One Solitary Life

He was born in an obscure village.
He worked in a carpenter shop until he was thirty.
He then became an itinerant preacher.
He never held office
He never had a family or owned a house.
He didn't go to college.
He had no credentials but himself.
He was only thirty-three when the public turned against him.

Nineteen centuries have come and gone, and today he is the central figure of the human race. All the armies that ever marched, all the navies that ever sailed, all the parliaments that ever sat, and all the kings that ever reigned have not affected the life of man on this earth as much as that *one solitary life*.

—Author Unknown

Time is slow when we are young, but as the years proceed–
Time steps out and seems to move twice its former speed–
Swiftly are the milestones passed, we see them flashing by–
Quickly do the birthdays come, time races– seasons fly.

With a shock we find that youth has fled and life half gone.
We should pause to look within before we hurry on–
Where exactly are we going? Where and why and how?
What if God should call us to account this moment–now.

Do not bank upon the future– It's not yours to plan.
No one but your maker knows the measure of your span.
We should always live each day as if it were the last–
The only chance to make amends for failings of the past.

—Author Unknown

Life, Talents, Time, Values

Beethoven's Moonlight Sonata

It happened at Bonn. One moonlight winter's evening I called upon Beethoven, for I wanted him to take a walk, and afterward sup with me. In passing through some dark, narrow street, he paused suddenly.

"Hush!" he said--"what sound is that? It is from my sonata in F!" he said eagerly. "Hark! how well it is played!"

It was a little, mean dwelling, and we paused outside and listened. The player went on; but in the midst of the finale there was a sudden break, then the voice of sobbing. "I cannot play any more. It is so beautiful, it is utterly beyond my power to do it justice. Oh, what would I not give to go to the concert at Cologne!"

"Ah, my sister," said her companion, "why create regrets, when there is no remedy? We can scarcely pay our rent."

"You are right; and yet I wish for once in my life to hear some really good music. But it is of no use."

Beethoven looked at me. "Let us go in," he said.

"Go in!" I exclaimed. "What can we go in for?"

"I will play to her," he said in an excited tone. "Here is feeling--genius--understanding. I will play to her, and she will understand it." And before I could prevent him his hand was upon the door.

A pale young man was sitting by the table making shoes; and near him, leaning sorrowfully upon an old-fashioned harpsichord, sat a young girl with a profusion of light hair falling over her bent face. Both were clearly but very poorly dressed, and both started and turned toward us as we entered.

"Pardon me," said Beethoven, "but I heard music, and was tempted to enter! I am a musician."

The girl blushed and the young man looked grave--somewhat annoyed.

"I-I also overheard something of what you said," continued my friend. "You wish to hear--that is, you would like--that is--Shall I play for you?"

There was something so odd in the whole affair, and something so comic and pleasant in the manner of the speaker, that the spell was broken in a moment, and all smiled involuntarily.

Life, Talents, Time, Values

"Thank you!" said the shoemaker, "but our harpsichord is so wretched, and we have no music.

"No music!" echoed my friend. "How, then, does the Fraulein--" He paused and colored up, for the girl looked full at him, and he saw that she was blind.

"I-I entreat your pardon!" he stammered. "But I had not perceived before. Then you play by ear?"

"Entirely."

"And where do you hear the music, since you frequent no concerts?"

"I used to hear a lady practicing near us, when we lived at Bruhl two years. During the summer evenings her windows were generally open, and I walked to and fro outside to listen to her."

She seemed shy; so Beethoven said no more, but seated himself quietly before the piano, and began to play. He had no sooner struck the first chord that I knew what would follow--how grand he would be that night. And I was not mistaken. Never, during all the years I knew him, did I hear him play as he then played to that blind girl and her brother. He was inspired; and from the distant when his fingers began to wander along the keys, the very tone of his instrument began to grow sweeter and more equal.

The brother and sister were silent with wonder and rapture. The former laid aside his work; the latter, with her head bent slightly forward, and her hands pressed tightly over her breast, crouched down near the end of the harpsichord, as if fearful lest even the beating of her heart should break the flow of those magical, sweet sounds. It was as if we were all bound in a strange dream, and only feared to wake.

Suddenly the flame of the single candle wavered, sank, flickered, and went out. Beethoven paused, and I threw open the shutters, admitting a flood of brilliant moonlight. The room was almost as light as before, and the illumination fell strongest upon the piano and player. But the chain of his ideas seemed to have been broken by the accident. His head dropped upon his breast; his hands rested upon his knees; he seemed absorbed in meditation. It was thus for some time.

At length the young shoemaker rose and approached him eagerly, yet reverently. "Wonderful man!" he said in a low tone, "who and what are you?"

Life, Talents, Time, Values

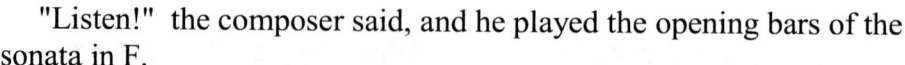

"Listen!" the composer said, and he played the opening bars of the sonata in F.

A cry of delight and recognition burst from them both, and exclaiming, "Then you are Beethoven!" They covered his hands with tears and kisses.

He rose to go, but we held him back with entreaties.

"Play to us once more--only once more!"

He suffered himself to be led back to the instrument. The moon shone brightly in through the window and lit up his glorious, rugged head and massive figure.

"I will improvise a sonata to the moonlight!" looking up thoughtfully to the sky and stars. Then his hands dropped on the keys, and he began playing a sad and infinitely lovely movement, which crept gently over the instrument like the calm of moonlight over the dark earth.

This was followed by a wild elfin passage in triple time--a sort of grotesque interlude, like the dance of sprites upon the sword. Then came a swift agitato finale--a breathless, hurrying, trembling movement, descriptive flight and uncertainty, and vague, impulsive terror, which carried us away on its rustling wings, and left us all in emotion and wonder.

"Farewell to you!" said Beethoven, pushing back his chair and turning toward the door--"farewell to you!"

"You will come again?" asked they in one breath.

He paused and looked compassionately, almost tenderly, at the face of the blind girl. "Yes, yes," he said hurriedly, "I will come again and give the Fraulein some lessons. Farewell! I will soon come again!"

They followed us in silence more eloquent than words, and stood at their door till we were out of sight and hearing.

"Let us make haste back," said Beethoven, "that I may write out that sonata while I can yet remember it."

We did so, and he sat over it till long past day--dawn.

And this was the origin of that moonlight sonata with which we are all so fondly acquainted.

–Author Unknown

Life, Talents, Time, Values

The Lord Had A Job For Me

The Lord had a job for me, but I had so much to do
I said, "You get someone else or wait 'til I get through."
I don't know how the Lord came out, no doubt he got along.
But I felt rather sneaking like, I knew I'd done God wrong.

One day I needed the Lord–needed him right away,
But He never answered me at all, and I could hear him say;
Down in my accusing heart, "Child I've too much to do.
You get someone else, or wait till I get through."

Now when the Lord has a job for me, I never try to shirk.
I drop what I have in hand and do the Lord's good work.
And my affairs can run along or wait 'til I get thru.
Nobody else can do the work the Lord has laid out for you.
—*Author Unknown*

A Piece Of Clay

I took a piece of clay
And idly fashioned it one day,
And, as my fingers pressed it still,
It moved and yielded to my will

I came again when days were past–
The bit of clay was hard at last;
The form I gave it, it still bore,
But I could change it no more.

I took a piece of living clay
And gently formed it day by day
And molded with my power and art
A young child's soft and yielding heart.

I came again when years were gone–
It was a man I looked upon;
He still that early impress wore,
And I could change him never more. —*Author Unknown*

Life, Talents, Time, Values

Life Is Largely What We Make It

Life surely is a see saw thing;
We never know just what 'twill bring,
Sometimes it lifts us "high in the air"
Where skies are blue, and all is fair;
Sometimes it "bumps" us down to earth
Mid gloomy days of little worth'
But never mind how dark the clouds
Nor blue the thoughts, that come in crowds.

    We know somewhere the sun is shining
    And every cloud hath silver lining;
    So lift your head, Throw out your chest,
    Put on a smile and do your best,
    Stand firm in will, there's naught can break it,
    For after all, life's what we make it.
                      –*Author Unknown*

The Clock Of Life

The clock of life is wound but once
    And no man has the power
To tell just where the hands will stop
    At late or early hour.

    Now is the only time you own.
        Live, Love, Toil, with a will
    Place no faith in tomorrow, for
        The clock may then be still.
              –*Author Unknown*

Life, Talents, Time, Values

Values of Life

Supposing today were your last on earth;
The last mile of the journey you've trod;
After all your struggles how much are you worth?
How much can you take home to God?

Don't count as possessions your silver or gold;
For tomorrow you leave them behind;
And all that is yours to have and to hold,
Are the blessings you've given mankind.

Just what have you done as you journeyed along;
That was really and truly worth while?
Do you think your good deed would offset the Wrong?
Could you look o'er your life with a smile?

We are only supposing, but if it were real,
And you invoiced your deeds since your birth;
And you figured the 'profits' you've made in life's deal:
How much are you really worth?
 –Author Unknown

There are two days in the week about which and upon which I never worry. Two carefree days, kept sacredly free from fear and apprehension. One of these days is Yesterday. . .and the other day I do not worry about is Tomorrow. —*Robert J. Burdette*

There are some things which cannot be learned quickly, and time, which is all we have, must be paid heavily for their acquiring. They are the very simplest things and because it takes a man's life to know them the little that each man gets from life is very costly and the only heritage he has to leave. —*Ernest Hemingway*

Life, Talents, Time, Values

How Do You Live Your Dash?

I read of a man who stood to speak
At a funeral of a friend...
He referred to the dates on her tombstone
From the beginning – to the end–
He noted that first came her date of birth
And spoke the following date with tears,
But he said what mattered most of all
Was the dash between those years (1900-1970)

For that dash represents all the time
That she spent alive on earth ...
And now only those who loved her
Know what that little line is worth...
For it matters not, how much we own;
The cars...the house...the cash,
What matters is how we live and love
And how we spent our dash–

So think about this long and hard...
Are there things you'd like to change?
For you never know how much time is left
That can still be rearranged.
If we could just slow down enough
To consider what's true and real,
And always try to understand
The way other people feel...

And be less quick to anger,
And show appreciation more
And love the people in our lives,
Like we've never loved before–
If we treat each other with respect,
And more often wear a smile...
Remembering that this special dash
Might only last a little while...

Life, Talents, Time, Values

So, when your eulogy's being read,
With your life's actions to rehash
Would you be proud of the things they say
About how you spent *YOUR DASH?*
—Author Unknown

The Wrong Way

I'll go where you want me to go dear Lord;
Real service is what I desire,
I'll do what you want me to do,
But don't ask me to sing in the choir.

I'll say what you want me to say dear Lord.
I love to see things come to pass,
But don't ask me to teach boys and girls,
I'd rather just stay in my class.

I'll do what you want me to do dear Lord,
I yearn for the Kingdom to thrive,
I'll give you my nickels and dimes dear Lord,
But please don't ask me to tithe.

I'll go where you want me to go dear Lord,
I'll say what you want me to say,
But I'm busy right now with myself dear Lord,
I'll help you some other day.
—Author Unknown

Socrates thought that if all our misfortunes were laid in one common heap, when everyone must take an equal portion, most persons would be content to take their own and depart.
—Plutarch

Life, Talents, Time, Values

This New Day

This brand new day is time to spend exactly as I choose
To mark with real accomplishment or squander and misuse
To fill with love and cheerfulness or bitterness and pain
It is my choice to make this day a total loss- - or gain
So counsel and direct me Lord that when this day shall end
I may rejoice at work well done, be richer by a friend
And when I sleep, may angels pause beside your throne and tell
That I have lived this day of mine not wastefully- - but well.
–*Author Unknown*

To everything there is a season, and a time to every purpose under the heaven:
A time to be born, and a time to die; a time to plant, and a time to pluck that which is planted;
A time to kill, and a time to heal; a time to break down, and a time to build up.
A time to weep, and a time to laugh; a time to mourn, and a time to dance;
A time to cast away stones, and a time to gather stones together;
A time to embrace, and a time to refrain from embracing;
A time to get, and a time to lose; a time to keep, and a time to throw away;
A time to rend, and a time to sew; a time to keep silence, and a time to speak; A time to love, and a time to hate; a time of war and a time of peace.-   –*Ecclesiastes 3:1-8*

Life, Talents, Time, Values

Then I Awoke

And in my dream I came to a beautiful building somehow like a bank, and yet not a bank because the brass marker said: *"Time for Sale."* I saw a man breathless and pale, painfully pull himself up the stairs like a sick man. I heard him say: "The doctor told me I was five years too late in going to see him. I'll buy those five years now and then he can save my life."

Then came another man, also older, to say to the clerk: "When it was too late, I discovered that God had given me great capacities and endowments, and I failed to develop them. Sell me ten years so that I can be the man I could have been."

Then came a younger man to say, "The company has told me that starting next month I can have a big job, if I am prepared to take it. But I'm not prepared. Give me two years of time so that I will be ready to take the job next month."

So they came, ill, hopeless, despondent, worried, unhappy- and they left smiling each man with a look of unattenable pleasure on his face for he had what he so desperately needed and wanted ... *"TIME"*.

Then I awoke, glad that I had what these men had not and what they could never buy- *TIME*, Time to do so many things I want to do, that I must do.

If that morning I whistled at my work, it was because a great happiness filled my heart. *For I still have TIME !   And so do you !*

–Author Unkown

Life, Talents, Time, Values

Time

The most priceless of all possessions is time.
Every second wasted can never be replaced.
Time is the most democratic of all properties.
Every human being is a millionaire at birth.
Everyone ends as a pauper in time.
What you buy with it depends on you.
Time can be exchanged for success or failure - -
which ever you prefer.
—*Author Unknown*

May You Have

Enough *happiness* to keep you sweet,
Enough *trials* to keep you strong,
Enough *sorrow* to keep you human'
Enough *hope* to keep you happy,
Enough *failure* to keep you humble,
Enough *success* to keep you eager,
Enough *friends* to give you comfort,
Enough *wealth* to meet your needs,
Enough *enthusiasm* to look forward,
Enough *faith* to banish depression,
Enough *determination* to make each day
better than yesterday.
—*Author Unknown*

Love, Sharing, Service, Sacrifice

Section 15

*If I can stop one heart from breaking,
I shall not live in vain;
If I can ease one life the aching,
Or cool one pain,
Or help one fainting robin
Unto his nest again,
I shall not live in vain.*
Emily Dickinson

Love, Sharing, Service, Sacrifice

Kindness

The greatest gifts you'll ever give
Though with them never part,
Are simply these: a helping hand,
And a selfless, loving heart.
—*Author Unknown*

Love is a great thing. . . which alone maketh every burden light. . . Love is watchful, and whilst sleeping still keeps watch; though fatigued, it is not weary, though pressed, it is not forced. . . Love is . . sincere. . gentle. . strong. . patient. . faithful. . prudent. . long-suffering..
—*Thomas A. Kempis*

If you're not satisfied with your lot in life, build a service station on it.
—*Author Unknown*

Only a life lived for others is a life worth while.   —*Albert Einstein*

What do we live for if not to make life less difficult for others?
—*George Eliot*

We tire of those pleasures we take, but never of those we give.
—*J. Petit*

There is a destiny that makes us brothers;
None goes his way alone;
All that we send into the lives of others
Comes back into our own.
—*Edwin Markham*

Love, Sharing, Service, Sacrifice

And whosoever will be chief among you, let him be your servant.
—Matt 20:27

In giving a man receives more than he gives, and the more is in proportion to the worth of the thing given. —George McDonald

He drew a circle that shut me out--
Heretic, rebel, a thing to flout.
But love and I had the will to win:
We drew a circle that took him in!
—Edwin Markham

A bell is no bell till you ring it,
A song is no song till you sing it.
And love in the heart isn't put there to stay,
Love isn't love...till you give it away.
—Author Unknown

Love is not getting, but giving...it is goodness,
and honor, and peace and pure living.
—Henry Van Dyke

Love, Sharing, Service, Sacrifice

Show You Care

Why wait till tomorrow
To do a good deed?
Someone's in trouble
Or maybe in need.

Offer a handshake,
Or just a kind smile
Make a short call
Or visit a while.

Many are lonely,
Some needing a friend,
Maybe life's ebbing
And nearing its end.

Pack up some kindness,
Get out and share
You'll make some happy
By showing you care.
–*Author Unknown*

The truest help we can render an afflicted man, is not to take his
burden from him, but to call out his best strength
that he may be able to bear the burden.
–*Phillips Brooks*

Greater love hath no man than this,
that a man lay down his life for his friends.
–*John 15:13*

Love, Sharing, Service, Sacrifice

Let Me Be A Little Kinder

Let me be a little kinder,
Let me be a little blinder,
To the faults of those about me
Let me praise a little more.

Let me be when I am weary,
Just a little bit more cheery,
Let me serve a little better
Those that I am striving for.

Let me be a little braver
When temptations bids me waver,
Let me strive a little harder
To be all that I should be.

Let me be a little meeker
To a brother that is weaker,
Let me think more of my neighbor
And a little less of me.
–*Author Unknown*

Light

The night has a thousand eyes,
And the day but one,
Yet the light of the bright world dies
With the dying sun.

The mind has a thousand eyes,
And the heart but one.
Yet the light of a whole life dies
When its love is done.[7]
–*Francis W. Bourdillon*

Love, Sharing, Service, Sacrifice

I'll Go, I'll Do, I'll Say, Dear Lord

I'll go where you want me to go dear Lord;
Real service is what I desire.
I'll do what you want me to do
But don't ask me to sing in the choir.

I'll say what you want me to say dear Lord.
I love to see things come to pass,
But don't ask me to teach boys and girls
I'd rather just stay in my class.

I'll do what you want me to do dear Lord,
I yearn for the kingdom to thrive,
I'll give you my nickels and dimes dear Lord,
But please don't ask me to tithe.

I'll go where you want me to go dear Lord,
I'll say what you want me to say,
But I'm busy right now with my self, dear Lord.
I'll help you some other day.
–Author unknown

I say unto you if ye should serve Him who has created you. . .and is preserving you from day to day. . . I say, if ye should serve Him with all of your whole soul yet ye would be unprofitable servants. . . All that He requires of you is to keep His commandments.
–Mosiah 2:21,22

Love, Sharing, Service, Sacrifice

The following inscriptions on the tombstones of two different men points out the ideal of Service:

> Here lies a miser who lived for himself,
> And cared for nothing but gathering pelf,
> Now, where he is, or how he fares
> Nobody knows and nobody cares.

> Sacred to the memory of General Charles George Gordon, who at all times and everywhere gave his strength to the weak, his substance to the poor, his sympathy to the suffering, his heart to God.

Footprints

One night a man had a dream and in his dream he reviewed the footsteps he had taken in his life. He looked and noticed that all over the mountains and difficult places that he had traveled there was one set of footprints; but over the plains and down the hills, there were two sets of footprints, as if someone had walked by his side.

He turned to Christ and said. "There is something I don't understand. Why is it that down the hills and over the smooth and easy places you have walked by my side; but, here over the tough and difficult places I have walked alone, for I see in those areas there is just one set of footprints."

Christ turned to the man and said, "It is that while your life was easy I walked along your side; but here, where the walking was hard and the paths were difficult, was the time you needed me most, and that is why *I carried you.*"

–Author Unknown

Love, Sharing, Service, Sacrifice

True Rest

Rest is not quitting
The busy career;
Rest is the fitting
Of self to one's sphere.

'Tis the brook's motion,
Clear without strife,
Fleeting to ocean,
After this life.

'Tis loving and serving,
The highest and best;
'Tis onward, unswerving,
And this is true rest.
—*Goethe*

A Plea

God grant me the strength to do some needed service here;
The wisdom to be brave and true the gift of vision clear
That in each task that comes to me
some purpose I may plainly see.

God teach me to believe that I am stationed at the post;
Although the humblest 'neath the sky, where I am needed most.
And that, at last, if I do well
my humble service will tell.

God grant me faith to stand on guard uncheered, unpraised, alone,
And see behind such duty hard my service to the throne.
What'er my task, be this my creed
I am on earth to fill a need.
—*Author Unknown*

Love, Sharing, Service, Sacrifice

The Bridge Builder

An old man traveling a long highway,
Came at the evening cold and gray,
To a chasm vast and deep and wide,
The old man crossed in the twilight dim,
The sullen stream held no fears for him;
But he turned when safe on the other side,
And built a bridge to span the tide.

"Old man," cried a fellow pilgrim near,
"You're wasting your time in building here.
Your journey will end with the closing day;
You never again will pass this way.
You have crossed the chasm deep and wide,
Why build you this bridge at even-tide?"

The builder lifted his old gray head;
"Good friend, in the path I have come," he said.
"There followeth after me today
A youth whose feet must pass this way,
This chasm which has been as naught to me,
To that fair-haired youth may a pitfall be;
He, too, must cross in the twilight dim--
Good friend, I am building this bridge for him."
  –Will Allen Dromgoole

The art of love is God at work, through you.
  –Wilfred A. Peterson

Love, Sharing, Service, Sacrifice

What Do We Plant

What do we plant when we plant the tree?
We plant the ship, which will cross the sea.
We plant the mast to carry the sails;
We plant the planks to withstand the gales...
The keel, the keelson, the beam, the knee;
We plant the ship when we plant the tree.

What do we plant when we plant the tree?
We plant the houses for you and me,
We plant the rafters, the shingles, the floors,
We plant the studding, the lath, the doors,
The beams and siding, all parts that be;
We plant the house when we plant the tree.

What do we plant when we plant the tree?
A thousand things that we daily see;
We plant the spire that out-towers the crag,
We plant the staff for our country's flag.
We plant the shade, from the hot sun free;
We plant all these when we plant the tree.
  –*Henry Abbey*

A Closing Thought

Did you stop to think
What makes a day seem bright?
It isn't just the bright sunshine,
Though, of course, that helps all right,
It's not just meeting friends you like.
Exchanging news, and jokes;
No sir, it's the little thoughtful things
You've done for other folks.
  –*Author Unknown*

Love, Sharing, Service, Sacrifice

The Day's Results

Is anybody happier
Because you passed his way,
Does anyone remember
That you spoke to him today?
This day is almost over,
And it's toiling time is through;
Is there anyone to utter now
A kind word of you?

Did you give a cheerful greeting
To a friend who came along;
Or a churlish sort of "Howdy"
And then vanish in the throng?
Were you selfish, pure and simple,
As you rushed along your way;
Or is someone really grateful
For a deed you did to-day?

Can you say tonight in parting,
With a day that's slipping fast.
That you helped a single brother
Of the many that you passed?
Is a single heart rejoicing
Over what you did and said?
Does a man whose hopes were fading
Now with courage look ahead?

Did you waste the day, or use it?
Was it well or poorly spent?
Did you leave a trail of kindness,
Or a scar of discontent?
As you close your eyes in slumber,
Do you think your God can say,
"You have earned one more tomorrow,
By the work you did today.
–Author Unknown

Suppose that today were your last day on earth,
The last mile of the journey you've trod;
After all of your struggles , how much are you worth,
How much can you take home to God?
Don't count as possessions your silver and gold
Tomorrow you leave these behind,
And all that is yours to have and to hold
Is the service you've rendered mankind.
–Author Unknown

Love, Sharing, Service, Sacrifice

My Heart Garden

The little blossom called content
Is in my garden growing,
And seeds of sweet unselfishness
In it I'm ever sowing.

Good-nature and the kindness flower
I've also planted there.
The truth and love are flourishing
Because I give them care.

Of course, the weed of laziness
And selfishness I know.
The temper plant, whose roots go deep
All these will try to grow.

But I will do my best to see
They do not get a start
For I want only flowers in
The garden of my heart.
  —*Author Unknown*

Do you wish the world were better?
Let me tell you what to do.
Set a watch upon your action
Keep them always straight and true.
Rid your mind of selfish motives,
Let your thoughts be clean and high,
You can make a little Eden
Of the spot you occupy
  —*Author unknown*

Love, Sharing, Service, Sacrifice

Do all the good you can
By all the means you can
In all the ways you can
To all the people you can
At all the Times you can
For as long as you can.
—*Author Unknown*

A closed hand cannot receive.
To receive love you must offer it.
—*Author Unknown*

O Master, let me walk with thee
In lowly paths of service free;
Tell me thy secret; help me bear
The strain of toil, the fret of care.

Help me the slow of heart to move
By some clear, winning word of love;
Teach me the wayward feet to stay
And guide them in the homeward way.

Teach me thy patience; still with thee
In closer, dearer company,
In work that keeps faith sweet and strong,
In trust that triumphs over wrong;

In hope that sends a shining ray
Far down the future's broadening way;
In peace that only thou canst give–
With thee, O Master, let me live!
—*Washington Gladden*

Love, Sharing, Service, Sacrifice

Oh Lord Bless Everyone

I knelt to pray when day was done.
And prayed, "O Lord bless everyone;
Lift from each saddened heart the pain
And let the sick be well again."
And then I woke another day
And carelessly went on my way.

The whole day long I did not try
To wipe a tear from any eye;
I did not try to share the load
Of any brother on my road;
I did not even go to see
The sick man just next door to me.

Yet once again when day was done
I prayed, "O Lord, bless everyone."
But as I prayed, into my ear
There came a voice that whispered clear:
"Pause, hypocrite, before you pray,
Whom have you tried to bless today?

God's sweetest blessings always go
By hands that serve him here below."
And then I hid my face, and cried,
"Forgive me, God, for I have lied;
Let me but see another day
And I will live the way I pray."
–*Whitney Montgomery*

Love, Sharing, Service, Sacrifice

Father Never Knew I Loved Him

The train was slowly leaving the station. I had with me a stack of magazines to read for the long journey home. But my eyes were filled with tears. I could not read. I had in my purse a telegram which said: "Father critically ill."

For the first time in my life, my father became a person, an individual. I recalled the years of my childhood, my teen-age years, my marriage. I was sad because I could not remember ever once having told my father in all those years that I loved him.

My father was a quiet man, a gentle-person with high ideals. He had worked hard to make life pleasant for his family. He had to travel a great deal and spent much of his time in small uncomfortable hotels when he was away from home. I remembered that when he was home, my sister and I never seemed to have time to spend with him.

As the train sped on I prayed that there might still be time for me to tell my father that I loved him. When I arrived home, I tip-toed into my fathers room. He opened his eyes, and for a moment it seemed to me that he recognized me. Then he was in a coma.

Through the long week that followed I sat by his bedside for hours, hoping consciousness would return to him for just a moment, that I might tell him to stay with us. Then one rainy night, he died in my arms, as quietly as he had lived. How I wish I had told my father how much I loved him.

After the funeral, I had the task of going through his traveling bag and his letters in search of any unpaid bills or any unfinished business. With aching heart I examined his wallet. It held a dollar bill, some receipts and a letter. A letter that brought tears to my eyes. It was from my cousin Joyce, it was dated three years previously. My cousin Joyce would have been about eleven years old then. It was written on notebook paper. It was worn and limp from much folding, so I knew it had been read and reread many times.

She was thanking him for a dollar he had sent her. "I hope you can come to see us again soon," she had said. *"You are a wonderful man, Uncle Mark, and I love you."*

Love, Sharing, Service, Sacrifice

For three years my father had carried that letter. I could see him in his hotel room reading the tender words. He was alone, gathering comfort from a brother's child. The comfort which his own daughter had never given to him.

I wish I had told my father how much I loved him. *But now it's too late for me, but how about you?*
 —*Author Unknown*

Planting a Garden

Many of us love a garden, yet most gardens are seasonal. Here is a garden each of us can plant and reap and harvest at all times.

First plant five rows of P's
1. Presence
2. Promptness
3. Preparation
4. Perseverance
5. Purity

Plant three rows of squash
1. Squash gossip
2. Squash criticism
3. Squash indifference

Plant five rows of lettuce
1. Let us be faithful to duty
2. Let us be unselfish and loyal
3. Let us be true to our obligations
4. Let us obey rules and regulations
5. Let us love one another

No garden is complete without turnips
1. Turn up for all meetings
2. Turn up with a smile
3. Turn up new ideas
4. Turn up with a determination to make everything count for something good and worthwhile.

—*Author Unknown*

Love, Sharing, Service, Sacrifice

The Rich Man and The Stone

Many years ago, there lived a rich man who wished to do something for the people of his village. First, however, he wanted to find out whether they deserved his help.

In the center of the main road into the village he placed a very large stone. Then he hid nearby and waited to see what would happen. Soon an old farmer passed with his cow.

"What fool put this big stone right in the center of the road?" said the farmer, but he made no effort to remove the stone. Instead, with some difficulty he passed around the stone and continued on his way. Another man came along, and the same thing happened; then another came, and another, etc. All of them complained about the stone in the center of the road, but not one of them took the time or trouble to remove it.

Toward evening, a young man came along. He was honest and hardworking. He saw the stone and said to himself, "The night will be dark. Some stranger or a neighbor will come along in the dark, stumble on the stone, and perhaps hurt himself."

The young man then began to remove the stone. He had to push and pull with all his strength to move it to one side. But imagine his surprise when under the stone, he found a bag full of money and this message. "The money is for the thoughtful person who removes this stone from the road. That person deserves help."

–Author Unknown

It's high time that the ideal of success should be replaced by the ideal of service.
–Albert Einstein

Love, Sharing, Service, Sacrifice

Night Watch

A nurse took the tired, anxious serviceman to the bedside. "Your son is here," she said to the old man. She had to repeat the words several times before the patient's eyes opened. Heavily sedated because of the pain of his heart attack, he dimly saw the man in the Marine Corps uniform standing outside the oxygen tent. He reached out his hand. The Marine wrapped his toughened fingers around the old man's limp ones, squeezing a message of love and encouragement. The nurse brought a chair so the Marine could sit along side the bed.

Nights are long in hospitals, but all through the night the young Marine sat there in the poorly lighted ward, holding the old man's hand and offering words of hope and strength. Occasionally, the nurse suggested that the Marine move away and rest a while. He refused.

Whenever the nurse came into the ward, the Marine was there, oblivious of her and the night noises of the hospital, the clanking of the oxygen tank, the laughter of night-staff members exchanging greetings, the cries and moans of other patients. Now and then she heard him say a few gentle words. The dying man said nothing, only held tightly to his son most of the night.

Along toward dawn, the patient died. The Marine placed on the bed the lifeless hand he had been holding and went to tell the nurse. While she did what she had to he waited. Finally, she returned. She started to offer words of sympathy, but the Marine interrupted her.

"Who was that man?" he asked.

The nurse was startled. "He was your father," she answered.

"No, he wasn't," the Marine replied. "I never saw him before in my life."

"Then why didn't you say something when I took you to him?"

"I knew right off there had been a mistake, but I also knew he needed his son, and his son just wasn't there. When I realized he was too sick to tell whether or not I was his son, I knew how much he needed me."

–Roy Popkin

Love, Sharing, Service, Sacrifice

The Bridge

There was once a big turntable bridge which spanned a large river. During most of the day the bridge sat with its length running up and down the river parallel with the banks, allowing ships to pass through freely on both sides of the bridge. But at certain times each day, trains would come along and the bridge would be turned sideways over the river to allow the trains to cross.

A switchman sat in a small shack on one side of the river where he operated the controls to turn the bridge and lock it into place as the train crossed. One evening as the switchman was waiting for the last train of the day to come, he looked off into the distance through the dimming twilight, and caught sight of the train's light. He stepped to the controls and waited until the train was within a prescribed distance when he was to turn the bridge. He turned the bridge into position, but to his horror, he found the locking control did not work. If the bridge was not locked securely into position, it would wobble back and forth at the ends when the train came onto it, causing the train to jump the track and go crashing into the river. This would be a passenger train with many people aboard.

He left the bridge, turned across the river, and hurried across to the other side where there was a lever which he could use to operate the lock manually. He would have to hold the lever back firmly as the train passed. He could hear the rumble of the train now, and took a strong hold on the lever, leaning backward to apply his weight to locking the bridge. He kept applying the pressure of his body to keep the mechanism locked. Many lives depended on one man's strength.

Then, coming across the bridge from the direction of his control shack he heard a sound which made his blood run cold: "Daddy, where are you?" His four-year-old son was crossing the bridge to look for him. His first impulse was to cry out to his son, "Run!" "Run!" but the train was too close. Those tiny legs would never make it across the bridge in time. The man almost left the lever to run and snatch up his son and carry him to safety, but he realized he could not get back to the lever. Either the people on the train or his son must die.

Love, Sharing, Service, Sacrifice

He took just a minute to make his decision. The train sped swiftly on its way, and no one aboard was even aware of the tiny, broken body thrown mercilessly into the river by the rushing train. Nor were they aware of the pitiful figure of a sobbing man, still clinging tightly to the locking lever long after the train had passed. They didn't see him walking home more slowly than he had ever walked before--to tell his wife how he had sacrificed her son.

–Author Unknown

Something to Think About

I did a favor yesterday, a kindly little deed.
And then I called to all the world to stop and look and heed.
They stopped and looked and flattered me in words I could not trust,
And when the world had gone away my good deed turned to dust.

A very tiny courtesy I found to do today;
'Twas quickly done, with none to see, and then I ran away...
But someone must have witnessed it, for–truly I declare–
As I sped back the stony path roses were blooming there!
–Author Unknown

When love and skill work together expect a masterpiece.
–John Ruskin

Love, Sharing, Service, Sacrifice

Experience Of Thomas Moore

My favorite love story is also a true one. Soon after he was married, Thomas Moore, the famous 19th century Irish poet, was called away on a business trip. Upon his return he was met at the door not by his beautiful bride, but by the family doctor.

"Your wife is upstairs," said the doctor. "But she has asked that you do not come up." And then Moore learned the terrible truth: his wife had contracted smallpox. The disease had left her once flawless skin pocked and scarred. She had taken one look at her reflection in the mirror and commanded that the shutters be drawn and that her husband never see her again. Moore would not listen. He ran upstairs and threw open the door of his wife's room. It was black as night inside. Not a sound came from the darkness. Groping along the wall, Moore felt for the gas jets.

A startled cry came from a black corner of the room. "No! Don't light the lamps!"

Moore hesitated, swayed by the pleading in the voice.

"Go!" She begged. "Please go! This is the greatest gift I can give you, now."

Moore did go. He went down to his study, where he sat up most of the night, prayerfully writing. Not a poem this time, but a song. He had never written a song before, but now he found it more natural to his mood than simple poetry. He not only wrote the words, but he wrote the music too. And the next morning, as soon as the sun was up he returned to his wife's room.

He felt his way to a chair and sat down. "Are you awake?" He asked.

"I am," came a voice from the far side of the room. "But you must not ask to see me. You must not press me, Thomas."

I will sing to you, then," he answered. And so for the first time, Thomas Moore sang to his wife the song that still lives today:

Love, Sharing, Service, Sacrifice

> Believe me, if all those endearing young charms,
> Which I gaze on so fondly today,
> Were to change by to-morrow, and fleet in my arms,
> Like fairy-gifts fading away,
> Thou wouldst still be adored, as this moment thou art,
> Let thy loveliness fade as it will,
> And around the dear ruin each wish of my heart
> Would entwine itself verdantly still.

Moore heard a movement from the dark corner where his wife lay in her loneliness, waiting. He continued—

> It is not while beauty and youth are thine own,
> And thy cheeks unprofaned by a tear,
> That the fervor and faith of a soul may be known,
> To which time will but make thee more dear!
>
> No, the heart that has truly loved never forgets,
> But as truly loves on to the close,
> As the sunflower turns to her god when he sets
> The same look which she turned when he rose!
>
> *–Thomas Moore*

The song ended. As his voice trailed off on the last note, Moore heard his bride rise. She crossed the room to the window, reached up and slowly drew open the shutters.

–Galen Drake

Love, Sharing, Service, Sacrifice

Two Seas In Palestine

There are two seas in Palestine. The Sea of Galilee and the Dead Sea. They are made from the same sparkling water of the river Jordan which flows down clear and cool from the heights of Hermon and the roots of the Cedars of Lebanon. Splashes of green adorn it banks. Trees spread out their thirsty roots to sip its healing waters. Fish are in abundance. It laughs in the sunshine and men build their houses near it. Every kind of life is happier because it is there.

Along its shores the children play as children played when He was there. He loved it. He could look across its silver surface when He spoke His parables. And on a rolling plain not far away He fed five thousand people. The Sea of Galilee has an outlet. Its gets to give. It gathers in its riches that it may pour them out again to fertilize the Jordan plains.

The river Jordan flows on south into the Dead Sea. Here is no splash of fish, no fluttering leaf, no song of birds, no children's laughter. Travelers choose another route unless urgent business. The air hangs heavy above its waters. And neither man, nor beast, nor foul will drink.

What makes this mighty difference in these neighboring seas? Not the river Jordan which empties the same good waters into both. Not the soil in which they lie, not the country 'round about. This is the difference: The Sea of Galilee receives but does not keep the Jordan. For every drop that flows into it, another drop flows out. It *gives and lives*. The giving and receiving go on in equal measure.

The Dead Sea with the same water is shrewder, hoarding its income jealously. It will not be tempted into generous impulses. Every drop it gets, it *keeps, it gives nothing*. The Dead Sea has no outlet.

As in life, there are two kinds of people in this world just as there are two seas in Palestine.

–Harry E. Fosdick

Love, Sharing, Service, Sacrifice

What The Spirit of Sunshine Means

"How's business, Eben?"

The old man was washing at the sink after his day's work.

"Fine. Marthy. Fine."

"Does the store look just the same? Land, how I'd like to be there again, with the sun shining in so bright! How does it look, Eben?"

"The store's never been the same since you left it, Marthy."

A faint flush came into Martha's cheeks. Is a wife ever too old to be moved by her husband's praise?

For years Eben and Martha had kept a tiny notion store. But one day Martha fell sick and was taken to the hospital.. That was months ago. She was out now, but she would never be strong again-never more be partner in the happy little store.

"I can't help hankering for a sight of the store," thought Martha one afternoon. "If I take it real careful, I think I can get down there. "Tisn't so far."

It took a long time for her to drag herself down-town but at last she stood at the head of the little street where the store was. All of a sudden she stopped. Not far from her on the pavement stood Eben. A tray hung from his neck. On this tray were arranged a few cards of collar-buttons, some papers of pins and several bundles of shoe-laces. In a trembling voice he called his wares.

Martha leaned for support against the wall of a building nearby. She looked over the way at the little store. Its windows were filled with fruit. Then she understood. The store had gone to pay her hospital expenses. She turned and hurried away as fast as her weak limbs would carry her.

"It will hurt him so to have me find it out!" she thought. And the tears trickled down her face.

"He's kept it a secret from me and now I'll keep it a secret from him. He sha'nt ever know that I know."

That night when Eben came in, chilled and weary. Martha asked cheerily the old question.

"How's business, Eben?"

"Better'n ever. Marthy." was the cheery answer, and Martha prayed God might bless him for his sunshiny spirit and love of her.

Ladies Home Journal 1903

Love, Sharing, Service, Sacrifice

The Legend of The Big Bell

In the ancient city of Peking stands the famous Big Bell, many times a man's height, cast during the glorious reign of the emperor Yung-lo. Of this most wonderful bell the following tale is told:

When the great Emperor Yung-lo had finished building the finest city in all Asia, Old Peking, he said, "Now, let there be cast a huge bell whose sweet voice shall float across the blue hills for a hundred *li*, north, south, east and west.

And so he summoned the master bell-maker, the one and only Kwan Yu. To him the Emperor said, "Make me this great bell without regard to its cost. Let it be said that it is the greatest and noblest under heaven."

So Kwan Yu started on his great work. Day and night he toiled unceasingly. For such a perfect bell he used the yellowest of gold, the whitest of silver, and the purest of iron that could be obtained from the body of Mother Earth. It would be his masterpiece.

The metal was melted in the roaring furnace and was cast in a great mold. But, alas, when it was taken out of it, many a crack appeared on its surface.

The great Kwan Yu started the work all over again; but the second time the bell came out imperfect. The gods must be displeased...

When the Emperor heard that the casting of his big bell had failed a second time, great was his impatience. Kwan Yu was summoned into his presence and bluntly told: "If you fail a third time, your head shall fall!" The heart of old Kwan Yu was sorely troubled, for he was afraid the third bell would also turn out badly.

Now, Kwan Yu had a daughter, the beautiful Ko Ngai, who saw the anxiety eating her old sire's heart. She must do something to help him. That night she secretly stole to the shadow of the city wall and there consulted an old soothsayer.

Love, Sharing, Service, Sacrifice

Said the soothsayer to the girl, "Your father's bell to be perfect must have the blood of a virgin mixed into the metal..."

The blood of a virgin...the blood of a virgin..." Repeated the girl as she walked home. The dutiful Ko Ngai had already decided how to save her dear father.

In the morning the third bell was to be cast, and her father was trembling in body and limb, fearing the uncertain outcome. But the smiling face of his beautiful daughter, standing by his side, seemed to lend him a certain courage.

The yellow flames of the furnace leapt and roared as if already mocking the old man with his failure. Suddenly a maiden's voice cut the silence: "For thy sake, O my father!" And the brave little Ko Ngai leapt into the boiling mass of metal.

Ko Ngai's maidservant had tried to stop her, but only succeeded in pulling away from the determined maiden one lone embroidered shoe of hers. O supreme sacrifice...

When the bell was tried, Hark! Its sweet, mellow voice floated over the blue hills for a full hundred *li,* for the sacred blood of a dutiful daughter had made it perfect.

In the olden days, when the Big Bell was struck in the cool evenings, the mellow tone would die among the distant hills of Peiping with a lingering *h-s-e-i-h*... note.

"Hark!" said the mothers telling the legend to the young ones, "Little Ko Ngai is crying for her shoe..."

–*Lim Sian-Tek*

Love, Sharing, Service, Sacrifice

I Lived Today

Let me today do something that will
Take a little sadness from the world's vast store;
And may I be so favored as to add to joy's
Too scanty sum, a little more.

Let me not hurt by word
Or deed, the heart of foe or friend
Nor would I pass unseeing worthy need,
Nor sin by silence I should defend.

However meager be my worldly wealth,
Let me give something that will aid my kind;
A word of hope, or thought of health,
Dropped as I pass, for troubled hearts to find.

Let me tonight look back across the span
'Twist dawn and dark, and to my conscience say:
Because of some good act to man or beast,
The world is better that I lived today.
—*Author Unknown*

You can give without loving,
but you can never love without giving.
—*Author Unknown*

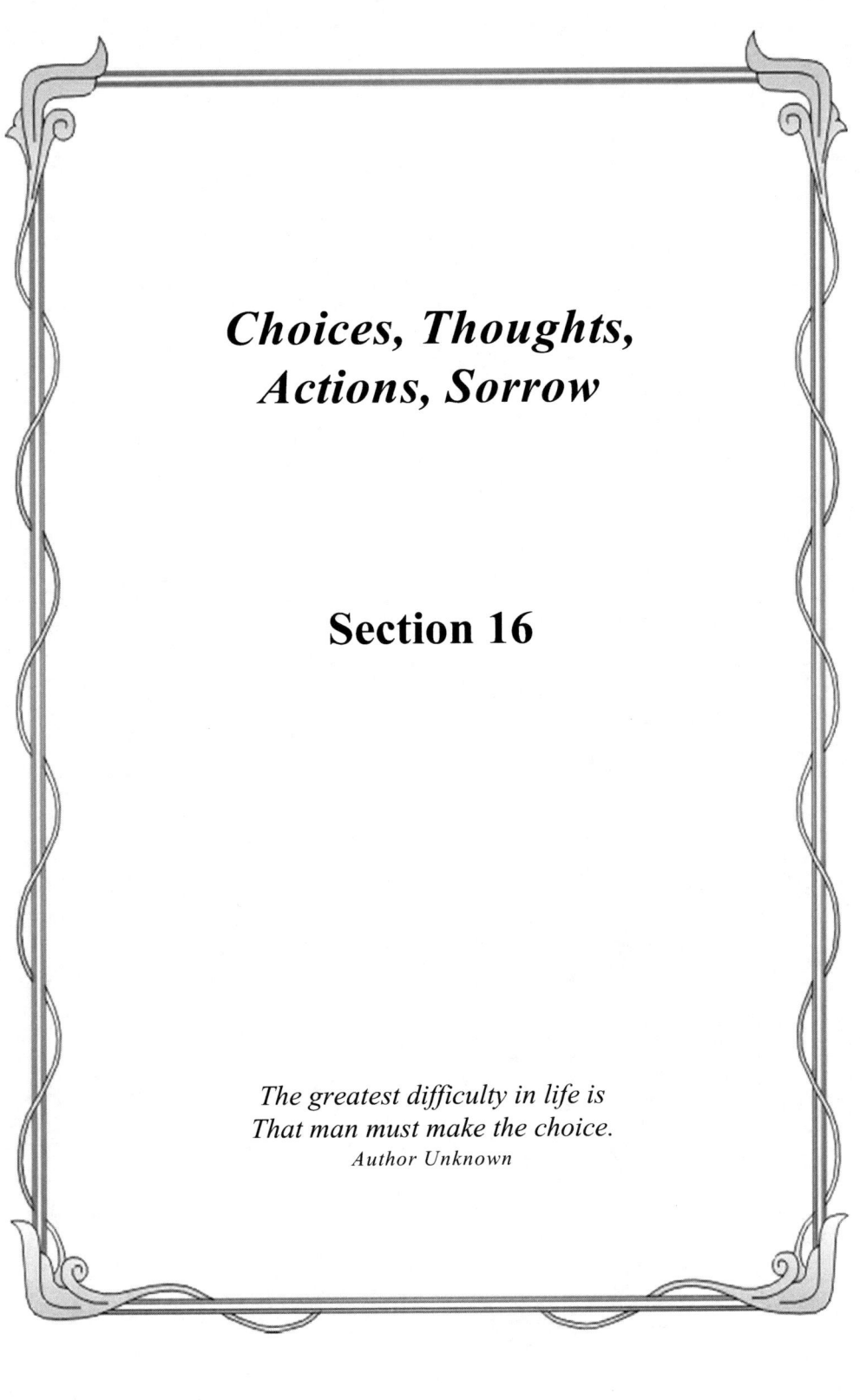

Choices, Thoughts, Actions, Sorrow

Section 16

*The greatest difficulty in life is
That man must make the choice.*
Author Unknown

Choices, Thoughts, Actions, Sorrow

Many of the luxuries, and many of the so-called comforts of life are not only not indispensable but positive hindrances to the elevation of mankind.
—*Henry David Thoreau*

Every man has his secret sorrows which the world knows not; and often-times we call a man cold when he is only sad.
—*Henry Wadsworth Longfellow*

Better keep yourself clean and bright,. You are the window through which you must see the world.
—*George Bernard Shaw*

The reputation of a thousand years may be determined by the conduct of one hour.
—*Japanese Proverb*

If we have not peace within ourselves, it is vain to seek it from outside.
—*Author Unknown*

Upon the valley's lap
The dewy morning throws
A thousand pearly drops
To wash a single rose.

So, often in the course
Of life's few fleeting years,
A single pleasure costs
The soul a thousand tears.
—*Frances W. Bourdillon*

Your success depends upon you.
You have to steer your own course.
You have to do your thinking.
You must make your own decisions.
You have to solve your own problems.
Your character is your handiwork.
You have to write your own record.
You have to build your own monument—or dig your own pit.
Which are you doing?
—*B.C. Forbes*

You live a long time with your memories, so make them good ones.
—*Author Unknown*

Choices, Thoughts, Actions, Sorrow

You cannot help men permanently by doing for them what they could and should do for themselves. *—James L. Phillips*

If I can stop one heart from breaking,
I shall not live in vain;
If I can ease one life the aching,
Or cool one pain,
Or help one fainting robin
Unto his nest again
I shall not live in vain.
—Emily Dickinson

While each of us..has depressed hours, none of us needs to be a depressed person.
—Henry Fosdick

He who wants to do a great deal of good at once will never do anything. Life is made up of little things. It is very rarely that an occasion is offered for doing a great deal at once. True greatness consist in being great in little things.
—C. Simmons

Choose you this day whom ye will serve. *—Joshua 24:15*

There is no pleasure in life equal to that of the conquest of a vicious habit.
—Author Unknown

Never lose an opportunity of seeing anything that is beautiful; for beauty is God's handwriting.
—Ralph Waldo Emerson

Repentance becomes more difficult as the sin is more willful,...
As the time of repentance is procrastinated, the ability to repent grows weaker,
—Author Unknown

Neglect of opportunity in holy things brings a forfeit of the chance.
—Author Unknown

Choices, Thoughts, Actions, Sorrow

We do not fully comprehend what we can do with our emotions. When we control them we have power. When they control us the results are often disastrous.
—*Norman Vincent Peal*

Blessed are the peacemakers: for they shall be called the children of God. —*Matthew 5:9*

Silence is the element in which great things fashion themselves together. —*Carlyle*

At the heart of the cyclone tearing the sky...is a place of central calm.
(The cyclone derives its power from a calm center. So does man.
—*Edwin Markham*

I wander through the still of night,
When solitude is ev'rywhere-
Alone, beneath the starry light,
And yet I know that God is there.
—*Theodore E. Curtis*

We are allowed a choice at every turn of the road...The Lord is ever willing to whisper in our ears which way we should turn.
—*Lindsay R. Curtis*

For time will teach thee soon the truth, There are no birds in last year's nest!
—*Henry Wadsworth Longfellow*

Each Day

Each day is like a clean new page
Without a single mark or spot;
But angry words or unkind deeds
Can mar it like an ugly blot.
I want to keep each page so white
That when at night I say my prayer
I'll surely hear the Master say,
"My child, this page is clean and fair." —*Author Unknown*

A sound discretion is not so much indicated by never making mistakes as by never repeating them. —*Boree*

Choices, Thoughts, Actions, Sorrow

The fundamental virtue of free agency is the right of each individual to choose.
—Author Unknown

Silence is sometimes an evidence of great courage.
—Author Unknown

For how many things, which for our own sake we should never do, do we perform for the sake of our friends.
—Cicero

The actions of men are the best interpreters of their thoughts.
—John Lock

That's Me, All Over

If I could live my life again, Have years back-just a few ones I wouldn't make the same mistakes. I might, though, make some new ones.
—Author Unknown

They are never alone that are accompanied with noble thoughts.
—Sir Philip Sidney

If you don't know where you are going—Any road will take you there.
—Author Unknown

The saddest words of tongue or pen are these four words: *It might have been.*
—Author Unknown

Our thoughts are blue prints of what we propose to do.
—Author Unknown

He who restrains his anger Overcomes his greatest enemy.
—Latin Proverb

He who chooses the beginning of a road chooses the place to which it leads.
—Author Unknown

Choices, Thoughts, Actions, Sorrow

Porch Swing

I cannot think of anything...
So lovely as my front porch swing,
Where I can go to slip away...
From all the heartaches of the day.

My swing is fastened to a star
In heaven where the angels are,
And often down to me, it seems
They bring a thousand little dreams.

And when upon my swing I sit
And very gently sway with it,
I often close my weary eyes
And think of you beneath these skies.

This swing of mine across the years
Has held my smiles and silent tears.
And all the loves of long ago
That in my youth I used to know.

I hope some night that you will be
Upon this front porch swing with me
And in the warm and soft blue air,
My comfort in the night time share.

–John C. Metcalfe

Choices, Thoughts, Actions, Sorrow

The Lost Chord

Seated one day at the organ,
   I was weary and ill at ease,
And my fingers wandered idly
   Over the noisy keys.

I know not what I was playing,
   Or what I was dreaming then:
But I struck one chord of music
   Like the sound of a great Amen.

It flooded the crimson twilight
   Like the close of an angel's psalm,
And it lay on my fevered spirit
   With a touch of infinite calm.

It quieted pain and sorrow,
   Like love overcoming strife:
It seemed the harmonious echo
   From our discordant life.

It linked all perplexed meanings
   Into one perfect peace,
And trembled away into silence
   As if it were loath to cease.

I have sought, but I seek it vainly,
   That one lost chord divine,
That came from the soul of the organ
   And entered into mine.

It may be that Death's bright angel
   Will speak in that chord again,
It may be that only in heaven
   I shall hear that grand Amen.

      –*Adelaide A. Proctor*

Choices, Thoughts, Actions, Sorrow

These things I have spoken unto you, that in me ye might have peace. In the world ye shall have tribulation, but be of good cheer, I have overcome the world. —*John 16:33*

The Two Words

One day a harsh word, rashly said
Upon an evil journey sped,
And like a sharp and cruel dart
It pierced a fond and loving heart;
It turned a friend into a foe,
And ev'rywhere brought pain and woe.

A kind word followed it one day,
Flew swiftly on its blessed way;
It healed the wound and soothed the pain,
And friends of old were friends again;
It made the hate and anger cease,
And everywhere brought joy and peace.

Oh! if we would but learn to know
How swift and sure one word can go,
How we would weigh, with utmost care,
Each thought before it sought the air,
And only speak the words that move
Like white-winged messenger of love.
—*Author Unknown*

Choices, Thoughts, Actions, Sorrow

Men Are Sometimes Just Like Trees

A popular tree grew tall and straight,
Like a mighty fire, near our barnyard gate
But then one day there came that way,
A careless man on a load of hay,
And the hayrack rubbed against the bark
And left a very ugly mark.

But long before the wound was healed,
Another crop was in the field
And soon there came that way again,
The careless man on a load of grain;
And again the rack dug through the bark,
And opened up the ugly mark.

Then winter's blast began to mar,
And insects crept within the scar,
And dry-rot took its toll like sin,
Until there was no heart within,
The outward tree looked just as well,
But its support was just a shell.

And when a brisk wind came one night,
The tree crashed down without a fight.
Men are sometimes just like trees,
Tobacco scars and drink disease.
They look as strong as men can be,
But deep within they're like the tree.

And if they're called to show their might,
They're apt to fold without a fight.
It's wisdom now, it seems to me,
That we should learn from this dead tree.
Avoiding paths where sin abound,
Will make men goodly, strong and sound.

                    –*Author Unknown*

Choices, Thoughts, Actions, Sorrow

Along The Road

I walked a mile with Pleasure
She chattered all the way,
But left me none the wiser
For all she had to say.

    I walked a mile with sorrow,
    And ne'er a word said she.
    And Oh, the things I learned from her
    When sorrow walked with me!
       –Robert Browning Hamilton

The Only Way

And if the road were easy,
   and if the burden light,
There'd be no need for courage,
   no cause to set things right.

    The desert sands are sunny,
      where seldom falls the rain,
    But beauty worth the having
      is grown by toil and pain.

        No way to pride through pleasure,
          no gate to strength through ease,
        Strict is the code of honor,
          life gives no cheap degrees.

            Knowledge is gained by study,
              patience, the will to work and wait,
            For these alone young fellow,
              can make you truly great.
                –Author Unknown

Choices, Thoughts, Actions, Sorrow

I Have Found Today

I've shut the door on yesterday,
Its sorrows and mistakes;
I've locked within its gloomy walls
Past failures and heartaches.
And now I throw the key away
To seek another room,
And furnish it with hope and smiles.
And every springtime bloom.

No thought shall enter this abode
That has a hint of pain,
And worry, malice and distrust
Shall never therein reign.
I'll shut the door on Yesterday
And throw the key away-
Tomorrow holds no doubts for me,
Since I have found Today.
    –Author Unknown

Watch your thoughts, they become your words,
Watch your words, they become your actions,
Watch your actions, they become your habits,
Watch your habits, they become your character,
Watch your CHARACTER.
    –Author Unknown

But I say unto you, Love your enemies, bless them that curse you, do good to them that hate, and pray for them which despitefully use you, and persecute you,"
    –*Matthew 5:44*

Choices, Thoughts, Actions, Sorrow

You Never Can Tell

You never can tell when you send a word
   Like an arrow shot from a bow
By an archer blind, be it cruel or kind,
   Just where it may chance to go.
It may pierce the breast of your dearest friend,
   Tipped with its poison or balm,
To a stranger's heart in life's great mart
   It may carry its pain or its calm.

You never can tell when you do an act
   Just what the result will be.
But with every deed you are sowing a seed,
   Though the harvest you may not see.
Each kindly act is an acorn dropped
   In God's productive soil;
You may not know, but the tree shall grow
   With shelter for those who toil.

You never can tell what your thought will do
   In bringing you hate or love,
For thoughts are things, and their airy wings
   Are swifter than carrier dove.
They follow the law of the universe-
   Each thing must create its kind,
And they speed o'er the track to bring you back,
Whatever went out from your mind.
                        –*Ella Wheeler Wilcox*

How Many Hurts

"Suppose," said I, "You chanced to see
A small boy tumble from a tree,
How would you tell that tale to me?"
"Why Dad," said he, "I'd simply say
I saw a boy get hurt today
And two men carried him away."

"How many injured would there be?"
I asked. "Just one, of course" said he
"The boy who tumbled from the tree."
"No, no," I answered him, "That fall
Which hurt the lad brought pain to all
Who knew and loved that youngster small.

"His mother wept, his father sighed,
His brothers and his sisters cried,
And all his friends were hurt inside.
"Remember this your whole life through–
Whatever hurts may come to you
Must hurt all who love you, too.

"You cannot, live your life alone,
We suffer with your slightest groan,
And make your pain or grief our own.
"If you should do one shameful thing,
You could not bear alone the sting,
We'd spend our years in suffering.

"How many hurt, we cannot state,
There never falls a blow of fate,
But countless people feel its weight.
-From "The Foreman."
–Author unknown

Choices, Thoughts, Actions, Sorrow

The Joy Of Living

If nobody smiled and nobody cheered,
    And nobody helped us along.
If each, every minute, looked after himself
    And the good things all went to the strong.
If nobody cared just a little for you,
    And nobody thought about me,
And we stood all alone in the battle of life,
    What a dreary old world it would be.

Life is sweet just because of the friends we have made,
    And the things which in common we share;
We want to live on, not because of ourselves,
    But because of the people who care.
It's giving and doing for somebody else—
    On that all life's splendor depends;
And the joy of this world, when
    You've summed it all up,
Is found in the making of friends.
    –Author Unknown

There is an old, old story told of a man from another planet who was permitted to visit the earth. From an eminence he looked down upon the bustling cities of the world. Millions of men, like ants, were busy building palaces of pleasure and other things that would not last; ... seeking financial bubbles that burst before their eyes. As he left to go back, he said, "All these people are spending their time in building just bird's nest, no wonder they fail and are ashamed." Peace does not come by seeking the superficial things of life.

    –Author Unknown

Choices, Thoughts, Actions, Sorrow

Choose Ye This Day!

Have you ever taken a light fixture down for cleaning and found dead insects inside in the bottom of the shade? The poor little creatures were attracted to the light only to be burned by its heat. They lacked the capacity to understand how something seemingly desirable would trap and harm them. Those creatures live their brief lives by instinct. But we have been given the gift of intelligence... We can foresee the consequences of our act. We can plan and manage our lives. We have been given the right to make choices, either which can help us go forward or hinder us as we travel thru' the Straight and Narrow Way. Knowing what is right and what we want and where we are going helps us to avoid the thing that could divert us from staying on the course.

We need wisdom in helping us to solve our own problems. We night be walking dictionaries, but if we don't develop the wisdom, and good judgement to solve our own problems, we won't be qualified to be president, or even manager of our own personal lives.

We need to use wisdom in learning new words. Words can make friends or enemies. Words have changed the course of history and individual lives. There are: kind words, cruel words, short words, long words, technical words and some we should use and others we should not. If we use wisdom, we can choose those words to help us and those words we should use.

Now is the time to develop wisdom and put it to use in our lives to develop goals, values, friends, ideals and standards.

–Author Unknown

Choices, Thoughts, Actions, Sorrow

'The Holy City'

Thirty men, red-eyed and disheveled, lined up before a judge of the San Francisco police court. It was the regular morning company of "drunks and disorderlies." Some were old and hardened, others hung their heads in shame. Just as the momentary disorder attending the bringing in of the prisoners quieted down, a strange thing happened. A strong, clear voice from below began singing:

> "Last night I lay a-sleeping,
> There came a dream so fair."

Last night! It had been for them all a nightmare or a drunken stupor. The song was such a contrast to the horrible fact that no one could fail of a sudden shock at the thought the song suggested.

> " I stood in old Jerusalem
> Beside the Temple there,"

The song went on. The judge had paused. He made a quiet inquiry. A former member of a famous opera company, known all over the country, was awaiting trial for forgery. It was he who was singing in his cell.

Meantime the song went on, and every man in the line showed emotion. One or two dropped on their knees: one boy at the end of the line, after a desperate effort at self-control, leaned against the wall, buried his face against his folded arms, and sobbed, "Oh mother, mother!"

The sobs cutting to the very heart of the men who heard, and the song, still welling its way through the court room, blended in the hush.

At length one man protested. "Judge," said he, "Have we got to submit to this? We're here to take our punishment but this"-- He too began to sob.

It was impossible to proceed with the business of the court, yet the judge gave no order to stop the song. The police sergeant, after an effort to keep the men in line, stepped back and waited with the rest. The song moved on to its climax.

> "Jerusalem, Jerusalem! Sing, for the night is o'er!
> Hosanna in the highest! Hosanna for evermore!"

In an ecstasy of melody the last words rang out, and then there was silence. The judge looked into the faces of the men before him. There was not one who was not touched by the song; not one in whom some better impulse was not stirred. He did not call the cases singly–a kind word of advice, and he dismissed them all. No man was fined or sentenced to the workhouse that morning. The song had done more good than punishment could possibly have accomplished.

–Author unknown

Man has two creators, his God and himself. The first creator furnishes him the raw material of his life–the laws and conformity with which he can make that life what he will. The second creator–himself–has marvelous powers he rarely realizes. It is what a man makes of himself that counts.
–William George Jordon

Only love can bring peace. Anyone who permits himself to hate any person, or any people, makes his own small but vital contribution towards the discord and trouble, while he who seeks to love others, even his enemies, makes his own priceless contribution to peace. . . .
The gift of peace on earth and good will to men was offered to the world in the gospel ... by our Savior. He made love of God and love of mankind fundamental, and declared, "On these two commandments hang all the law and the prophets."

Matthew 22:40

Choices, Thoughts, Actions, Sorrow

Barnacles

It is not uncommon to see ships of many different nations unloading and loading cargo on the docks at Portland, Oregon. To the passer-by it may seem strange because Portland is nearly 100 miles from the Pacific Ocean. Navigating this long trek up the Columbia and Willamette Rivers is difficult because of the turbulent passage over the bar guarding the Columbia River.

Why then do ship captains make this risky journey to dock at Portland. The answer is very understandable for one familiar with sea travel. A curious shellfish called a barnacle found only in saltwater fastens itself to a ship's hull. It will stay there for the rest of its life surrounding itself with a rock-like shell.

As a ship moves through the salt water more and more barnacles attach themselves. This increases the ship's drag thus slowing its movement which decreases the efficiency of the ship.

Therefore, the captain must take his ship periodically into dry dock so the barnacles can be scraped or chiseled off. This is a difficult, expensive, process that can tie up the ship for days.

However barnacles can not live in fresh water, so the captain maneuvers his ship to the sweet, fresh water of the Willamette or Columbia Rivers where the barnacles loosen and fall away. The ship can return to its task lightened and renewed without much delay.

To present an analogy, "sins" are like those barnacles. Few if any of us pass through life without picking up some. Sins as barnacles impedes
our progress, decreases our spirituality often for a life time. Without repentance they will eventually sink our soul.

A "viewpoint" article Church News Section of the Desert News.

Choices, Thoughts, Actions, Sorrow

Equal Inheritance

A certain merchant had two sons. The elder son was his favorite, and he intended to leave all his wealth to this son when he died. The mother felt sorry for her younger son, and she asked her husband not to tell the boys of his intention. She hoped to find some way of making her sons equal. The merchant heeded her wish and did not make known his decision.

One day the mother was sitting at the window weeping. A traveler approached the window and asked her why she was weeping.

"How can I help weeping?" she said. "There is no difference between my two sons, but their father wishes to leave everything to one and nothing to the other. I have asked him not to tell them of his decision until I have thought of some way of helping the younger. But I have no money of my own, and I do not know what to do in my misery."

Then the traveler said to her, "There is help for your trouble. Tell your sons that the elder will receive the entire inheritance, and that the younger will receive nothing. Then they will be equal."

The younger son, on leaning that he would inherit nothing, went to another land, where he served his apprenticeship and learned a trade. The elder son lived at home and learned nothing, knowing that some day he would be rich.

When the father died, the elder son did not know how to do anything and spent all his inheritance. However, the younger son, who had learned how to make money in a foreign country, became rich.

–Leo Tolstoy

Choices, Thoughts, Actions, Sorrow

Beware

A Chinese legend describes how the father of Sin decided to have a sale and dispose of all his tools to any one who would pay his price.

The implements were laid out in a row for inspection and among others were tools labeled "Malice," "Envy," "Hatred," "Jealousy," and "Deceit." Each one had a price tag on it. Apart from the others lay a harmless looking wedge-shaped tool, very much work from use, that was priced a great deal higher than the rest.

One of the buyers asked Satan what it was. "That," he answered, "is discouragement and it's in fine shape."

"But why have you priced it so high?"

"Because it is more useful to me than any of the others. I can pry open and get inside a man's consciousness with that wedge when I couldn't get near him with any of the others. And believe me once I do get inside I can use that man in whatever way suits me best. Of course, you'll notice it is well worn. That's because I use it with nearly everybody, for very few of you mortals know that it belongs to me."

However, the price was so high that this particular tool was never sold. Satan still owns it and is still using it.

–Author Unknown

A bend in the road is not the end of the road,
    unless you fail to make the turn.   –Author Unknown

Teacher, Teaching, Education

Section 17

*A house without books
is like a room without windows.*
Horace Mann

Teacher, Teaching, Education

If a teacher influences but one, his influence never stops.
—*Greek*

The creation of a thousand forests is in one acorn.
—*Ralph Waldo Emerson*

Education does not commence with the alphabet. It begins with a mother's look and a father's nod and a sister's gentle pressure on the hand and a brother's act of forbearance. With flowers and green dells and on hills with birds' nests admired but not touched, with pleasant walks in shady lanes, with thoughts directed in sweet and kindly tones, with deeds of virtue and benevolent thoughts to the source of all good and to God himself.
—*Author unknown*

If a man neglects education, he walks lame to the end of his life.
—*Author Unknown*

As long as you live, Keep learning how to live.
—*Seneca*

To the *Three R's*, namely Reading, -Riting and -Rithmetic; We need to add a *fourth- Responsibility*.
—*Herbert Hoover*

He who learns but does not think, is lost. He who thinks but does not learn, is in great danger.
—*Confucius*

If a carpenter, or a blacksmith should spoil a piece of material he is working upon, he could throw it aside and take another piece, but the teacher cannot do this with the eternal soul of a child
—*Karl G. Measer*

All who have meditated on the art of governing mankind have been convinced that the fate of empires depends upon the education of youth.
—*Aristotle*

Get wisdom: and with all thy getting, get understanding.
—*Proverbs 4:7*

Teacher, Teaching, Education

I'd laugh today, today is brief,
I would not wait for anything;
I'd use today that cannot last,
Be glad today and sing.
–Author unknown

How many a man has dated a new era in his life from the reading of a book.
–Henry David Thoreau

When you find that a book is poor...waste no more time upon it.
–James Bryce

You may have tangible wealth untold; caskets of jewels and coffers of gold. Richer than I you can never be–I have a mother who read to me.
–Strickland Gillilan

No ray of sunshine is ever lost but the green which it awakens takes time to sprout , and it is not always granted to the sower to see the harvest.
–Schweitzer

Seek ye out of the best books words of wisdom; seek learning, even by study and also by faith.
–D&C 88:118

Invest in a human soul. It may be a diamond in the rough.
–Mary McLeod Bethune

Happy is the man that findeth wisdom, and the man that getteth understanding.
For the merchandise of it is better than the merchandise of silver, and the gain thereof than fine gold.
–Proverbs 3:13-14

Learning is a treasure which will follow its owner everywhere.
–Chinese Proverb

Teacher, Teaching, Education

A child cannot be taught by anyone who despises him. And a child cannot afford to be fooled.
—*Socrates*

Everybody is ignorant, only on different subjects.
—*Will Rogers*

If you graduated yesterday, and have learned nothing today, you will be uneducated tomorrow.
—*Author unknown*

There are many things that go to make up an education, but there are just two things without which no man can ever hope to have an education, These two things are *Character and Good Manners*.
—*Dr. Nicholas Butler*

If you think education is expensive, try ignorance.
—*Derek Bok*

Education is growth–education is not just a preparation for life; Education is life itself.
—*John Dewey*

Wisdom is the power which enables you to use your knowledge to advantage.
—*Thomas Watson*

Ignorance is dangerous, but knowledge without responsibility is more dangerous.
—*Bruce B. Clark*

Education ought to foster the wish for truth. Men are born ignorant, not stupid. They are made stupid by education.
—*Bertrand Russell*

Education is not just in the filling of a pail; it is the lighting of a fire.
—*B.F. Skinner*

Education has produced a vast population able to read, but unable to distinguish what is worth reading.
—*G.M. Trevelyan*

Teacher, Teaching, Education

Knowledge is the eye of desire and can become the pilot of the soul. —*Will Durant*

If a man neglects education, he walks lame to the end of his life. —*Plato*

The man who does not read good books has no advantage over the man who can't read them. —*Mark Twain*

You cannot teach a man anything. You can only help him to find it within himself. —*Galileo*

Education is learning the rules, experience is learning the exceptions. —*Galileo*

To educate a man in mind and not in morals is to educate a menace to society. —*Theodore Roosevelt*

The object of true education is to make people not merely do the right things, but enjoy the right things— not merely industrious, but to love industry,— not merely learned, but to love knowledge— not merely pure but to love purity— not merely just but to hunger and thirst after justice. —*John Ruskin*

He who knows not,
and knows not that he knows not,
is a *fool*, Shun him!

He who knows not,
and knows that he knows not,
is *simple*, Teach him!

He who knows
and knows not that he knows,
is *asleep*, Waken him!

He who knows,
and knows that He knows,
is *wise*, Follow him!. —*Edward S. Ufford*

Ignorance is the night of the mind, but a night without moon or star. —*Confucius*

Teacher, Teaching, Education

The Teacher

Lord, Who am I to teach the way
To little children day by day
So prone myself to go astray?

I teach them KNOWLEDGE,
but I know
How faint they flicker and how low
The candles of my knowledge glow.

I teach them POWER
to will and do
But only now to learn anew
My own great weakness
through and through.

I teach them LOVE
for all mankind
And all God's creatures, but I find
My love comes lagging far behind.

Lord, if their guide I still must be,
Oh, let the little children see
The teacher leaning hard on Thee.
—*Author Unknown*

Whoso neglects learning in his youth loses the past,
and is dead for the future.
—*Euripides*

The basic ingredient of teaching always has been and always will be LOVE. When love comes first, the rest will follow in proper order. Without love we struggle in vain with all we do.
—*Author unknown*

That which we learn pleasantly we retain.
—*Galileo*

What school, college, or lecture bring to men depends on what men bring to carry it home in.
—*Ralph Waldo Emerson*

I'd leave all the hurry,
The noise and the fray,
For a house full of books
And a garden of flowers.
—*Andrew Lang*

Teacher, Teaching, Education

The Land Of Story Books

At evening when the lamp is lit,
Around the fire my parents sit;
They sit at home and talk and sing,
And do not play at anything.

Now, with my little gun, I crawl
All in the dark along the wall,
An follow round the forest track
Away behind the sofa back.

There, in the night, where none can spy,
All in my hunter's camp I lie,
And play at books that I have read
Till it is time to go to bed.

There are the hills, these are the woods,
These are my starry solitudes;
And there the river by whose brink
The roaring lions came to drink.

I see the others far away
As if in fire lit camp they lay,
And I, like to an Indian scout,
Around their party prowled about

So, when my nurse comes in for me,
Home I return across the sea,
And go to bed with backward looks
At my dear Land of Story Books.

–Robert Louis Stevenson

Teacher, Teaching, Education

A Diamond In The Rough

A diamond in the rough is a diamond, sure enough,
And before it ever sparkled it was made of diamond stuff.
But someone had to find it or it never would be found,
And someone had to grind it or it never would be ground.

But it's found, and when it's ground,
And when it's burnished bright,
That diamond's everlastingly giving out its light.

O teachers of our young folk,
Don't say you've done enough;
It may be that your rudest is
A diamond in the rough.
  —*Author unknown*

Asked what he thought should be taught to children first, *Samuel Johnson* replied that "It is no matter what you teach them first, any more than what leg you shall put into your britches first. Sir, you may stand disputing which is best to put in first, but in the mean time your breech is bear. Sir, while you are considering which of two things you should teach your child first, another boy has learnt them both."

I have walked with people whose eyes are full of light but who see nothing in sea or sky, nothing in city streets, nothing in books. It were far better to sail forever in the night of blindness with sense, and feeling, and mind, than to be content with the mere act of seeing. The only lightless dark is the night of darkness in ignorance and insensibility.
  —*Helen Keller*

Teacher, Teaching, Education

The Light Of My Love

I cannot watch you all of the way
Holding your hand as I do now,
To keep you from falling or from getting lost
Guarding your safety at whatever cost—
You will have grown to adulthood in such a little day!

Nor will you want my guidance any more,
So eager will you be to walk alone.
May I be wise to teach you how to go,
To look at life with clear undaunted eyes.
What things to value—which ones to despise;
How to have courage in the darkest night,
And strength for all the hardships you may know.

Teach you how to love—and how to pray—
Then, though you do not have my hand
To hold, you will have learned,
How to walk safely by yourself instead—
Because I cannot watch you all the way
My love must throw its light far, far, ahead.
—Author unknown

An individual learns best those things that he wants to learn...

...best those things he is able to do.

...best those things that tie in with what is familiar to him.

...most effectively those thing that make sense to him.

...best when he takes part in the learning process.

...most effectively when he knows what he is doing

...best when he gets satisfaction out of the learning process.
—Author unknown

Teacher, Teaching, Education

First Day Of School

It was the first day of a new school year.
And as I sat there pondering,
A youth stood in the framework of the door.
Of what he came to ask I do no know.
I sat transfigured before his tattered form.

Unruly hair defied a left-hand pass
Swung 'cross his brow to keep it from his eyes.
His Levis, hanging over narrow hips,
Were low upon his shoes and covered up his slouching socks.
And here and there his shirt and denim pants had parted company.

And again that tousled mop defied a pass,
And as he made that pass I saw his eyes.
And deep within I saw a prophet there
Who rose to lead the people to the light!
I saw a statesman plan a better world!
I saw a Saint whose life was clean and pure!

Or did I see, down deep within those eyes,
A devil lurking there whose fiendish power
Would wrought upon an unsuspecting world,
The havoc of destruction— slavery,
Satanic evils of barbarity!

What shall he be— devil, prophet, Saint?
Who shall determine what his destiny?
With such a challenge, who am I to shirk?
There stands my mission, framed within the door.
What of bank accounts and lands to me?
Are they the objects of my strivings here,
As forth I walk to show this youth the way?

Nay, Verily, my job is not a job,
For I determine this boys's destiny!
–J. Karl Wood

Teacher, Teaching, Education

Two Temples

A builder builded a temple,
He wrought it with grace and skill;
Pillars and groins and arches
All fashioned to work his will.
Men said as they saw its beauty,
"It shall never know decay;
Great is thy skill, O builder!
Thy fame shall endure for aye."

A teacher builded a temple
With loving and infinite care,
Planning each arch with patience,
Laying each stone with prayer.
None praised her unceasing efforts,
None knew of her wondrous plan,
For the temple the teacher builded
Was unseen by the eyes of man.

Gone is the builder's temple,
Crumpled into the dust;
Low lies each stately pillar,
Food for consuming rust.
But the temple the teacher builded
Will last while the ages roll,
For that beautiful unseen temple
Was a child's immortal soul.
　　　　　–*Hattie Rose Hall*

Teacher, Teaching, Education

The Learned Son

A learned son from the city one summer day returned to the country to visit his father. "Today we are moving the hay," Said the father. "Take a rake and help me."

The son did not want to work out in the hot sun, so he replied, "I am now a scholar and I have forgotten all those lowly peasant words." Walking arrogantly across the yard, he stepped on a rake that was lying in his way. It struck him hard on his forehead. Clutching his aching head he suddenly seemed to recall what a rake was and cried out, "What fool left a rake lying here?"

—*Leo Tolstoy*

I saw tomorrow passing on little children's feet
And on their forms and faces her prophecies complete
And then, I saw tomorrow look at me through little children's eyes,
And I thought how carefully I must teach, if I am wise.

—*Author unknown*

Character is higher than intellect.
A great soul will be fit to live as well as to think.
—*Ralph Waldo Emerson*

The primary concern of American education today is not the development of the appreciation of the "good life" in young gentlemen... Our purpose is to cultivate the largest possible number of our future citizens an appreciation of both the responsibilities and the benefits which come to them because they are Americans and are free.

—*James Bryant Conant* (Howard Univ. 1944)

The Unmailed Letter

Dear Teacher,

Today at commencement we had a peach of an address, "The Education I Wish I Might Have Had." It made me think. And I'm going to break loose and tell you about memories some fellows have which I haven't had.

I wish I could remember one morning that you greeted me with a happy smile when I walked into the room. It would have made such a bright beginning for the day. I know that I wasn't much to look at with my brown freckled face crowned with a mop of red hair that just wouldn't stay down no matter how often I combed it. And my ears--that's why they were always so dirty–they were so big, and they stuck straight out catching every particle of dirt that the wind swept by. My clothes were dirty too, but that wasn't altogether my fault. Mother never did feel well after baby Sally was born, and I could always dirty my clothes faster than she could get around to wash them. I can hear Mother say in her tired voice: "Johnny, how do you ever get so dirty?" She promised me she would wash my trousers after I had gone to bed, (I only had one pair) but I guess she was just too tired after putting Sally to bed and then tucking in Billy and Bob, the twins, and Mary, Jane, Tommy, and me for the night before leaving to hunt for Dad who would be in any one of the six Taverns.

You can't imagine how much your smile would have meant on some of these mornings that I came to school with only a dry crust of bread for my breakfast. Once or twice I thought you were going to smile--and then, you just said in a stern voice: "John, You're late again, as usual." That "as usual" as an afterthought always cut like a knife, and that's why I was afraid you wouldn't understand if I told you the real reason why I was late. Baby Sally needed the milk, and I used to walk the three miles over to Smith's every morning to get it. He sold us the milk two cents cheaper than Mr. Jones who lived just across the lane from us.

I wish I could remember one kind word that you spoke to me directly, Or one time when we played games that you joined the circle next to me and took my hand like you did the other boys'. True, my hands always looked

Teacher, Teaching, Education

dirty.–it's hard to wash in cold well-water with no soap–but if I'd have known there was a chance that you would take hold of my hand, I'd have scrubbed and scrubbed until they had been clean. The only time you seemed to notice me was when I pulled Norma's hair or poked Bonnie with my pencil. No one wanted to play with me, and sometimes I just felt like I had to do something to make sure I was still there.

I wish I could remember one time that you included me in the planning of the class work, instead of simply ignoring me. I rebelled at that–not at the work itself, as you supposed when I caused a disturbance or did everything except the work I was supposed to do–but because you didn't consider my views or reasons.

I wish I could remember, above all else, just one time that you and I talked together alone discussing my problems, so that you could have had a better understanding of why I had to do some of the things I did. It was always so easy for you to solve any problem that came up in class, and I'm sure that you could have helped me with my own problems and troubles. Please do not think I am blaming you. No teacher could ever have worked harder and had the children's welfare more at heart than you did.

No one could have taught me better how to work, or set a better example of honesty, industry and clean living. But you just didn't know that I, too, dirty and late as I was, needed those things that you had with you all the time–things that you gave freely to others but withheld from me. You couldn't have been better to me–no teacher could–but surely, you could have been infinitely nearer.

Your one time pupil,

P.S. I can't send this. After all these years you wouldn't understand. But I wish you knew that I'd gladly give my four years at college for the memories I might have had.

–C. J. Wendell

Teacher, Teaching, Education

Ten Commandments For The Teacher

1. <u>Thou shalt make the child the center of thy teaching.</u> Five days each week shalt thou help him to develop the best in his own personality.

2. <u>Thou shalt provide opportunities for experience learning,</u> not doing difficult tasks for the child but rather helping him to do them himself.

3. <u>Thou shalt set before him high attainable ideals,</u> surrounding him with the things that inspire thought, and encouraging him to cultivate a love for the good and true.

4. <u>Thou shalt help him to achieve success,</u> attempting not those tasks which are beyond his mental and physical ability but rather discovering within his natural ability that which he can do well.

5. <u>Thou shalt teach him to create, not copy,</u> for thou knowest the pride that is in thine own breast when thou doest something original.

6. <u>Thou shalt help him to develop the art of living happily with others</u>, by being kind, courteous, and considerate of his friends and associates.

7. <u>Thou shalt teach him to make wise choices,</u> permitting him to decide many issues for himself and requiring him to live by his decisions.

8. <u>Thou shalt talk with him as a friend,</u> remembering that love correcteth better than anger.

9. <u>Thou shalt speak kindly to him,</u> for thou knowest that there can be kindness in firmness.

10. <u>Thou shalt help him to find happiness in play,</u> so that he will learn that those who play fair and enjoy playing are the real winners.

–Author Unknown

Teacher, Teaching, Education

Sculpturing

I dreamed I stood in a studio
And watched two sculptors there,
The clay they used was a young child's mind
And they fashioned it with care.

One was a teacher; the tools he used
were books, music and art;
One, a parent, who worked with a guiding
Hand, and a gentle, loving heart.

Day after day the teacher toiled,
With touch that was deft and sure,
While the parent labored by his side
And polished and smoothed it o'er.

And when at last their tasks were done,
They were proud of what they had wrought,
For the things they had molded into the child
Could neither be sold nor bought.

And each agreed that he would have failed
If he had worked alone,
*For behind the teacher stood the school,
And behind the parent, the home.*
—Author Unknown

Teacher, Teaching, Education

Judith Swanson tells about how she learned a great lesson:

> From the day we entered the ninth-grade health class, one blackboard was covered with the names and locations of the major bones and muscles of the human body. The diagram stayed on the board through the term, although the teacher never referred to it. The day of the final exam, we came to class to find the board wiped clean. The sole test question was: "Name and locate every major bone and muscle in the human body."
>
> The class protested in unison: " We never studied that !"
>
> "That's no excuse," said the teacher. "The information was there for months." After we struggled with the test for a while, he collected the papers and tore them up. "Always remember," he told us, "that *education is more than just learning what you are told.*"

> Each day I learn more than I teach;
> I learn that half knowledge of another's life
> Leads to false judgment;
> I learn that there is a surprising kinship in human nature;
> I learn that it's a wise father who knows his own son;
> I learn that what we expect we get;
> I learn that there is more good than evil in this world;
> That age is a question of spirit;
> That youth is the best of life;
> No matter how numerous its years;
> I learn how much there is to learn.
>   –Virginia Church

Forgiving, Tolerance, Mercy, Greed

Section 18

*He that cannot forgive others,
Breaks the bridge over which he must pass himself,
For every man hath need to be forgiven.
--E. Herbert*

Forgiving, Tolerance, Mercy, Greed

A man who has committed a mistake and doesn't correct it is committing another mistake.
—*Confucius*

Sin is not hurtful because it is forbidden, but it is forbidden because it is hurtful.
—*Benjamin Franklin*

Somebody

Somebody did a golden deed;
Somebody proved a friend in
   need;
Somebody sang a beautiful song;
Somebody smiled the whole day
   long;
Somebody thought, "'Tis sweet to
   live";
Somebody said, "I'm glad to
   give";
Somebody fought a valiant fight;
Somebody lived to shield the
   right;
   Was that "somebody" you?
—*Author Unknown*

Every task, however simple
   Sets the soul that does it, free;
Every deed of love and mercy
   Done to man, is done to me.
—*Henry Van Dyke*

Folks And Me

It is a funny thing, but true,
That folks you don't like, don't
   like you.
I don't know why this should be
   so,
But just the same I always know
If I am 'sour,' friends are few;
If I am friendly, folks are too.
Sometimes I get up in the morn
A-wishin' I was never born.
I make of cross remarks a few,
And then my family wishes too
That I had gone some other place
Instead of showin' them my face.
But let me change my little tune
And sing and smile, then pretty
   soon
The folks around me sing and
   smile
I guess 'twas catchin' all the
   while.
Yes, 'tis funny, but it's true,
That folks you like will sure like
   you.
—*Author Unknown*

Teach me to feel another's woe,
To hide the faults I see,
That mercy, I to others show,
That mercy show to me.
—*Alexander Pope*

Forgiving, Tolerance, Mercy, Greed

Forgetting

If you were busy being *kind,*
Before you knew it you would find
You'd soon forget to think 'twas true
That someone was unkind to you.

If you were busy being *glad*
And cheering people who seem sad,
Although your heart might ache a bit,
You'd soon forget to notice it.

If you were busy being *good,*
And doing just the best you could,
You'd not have time to blame some man
Who's doing just the best he can.

If you were busy being *true,*
To what you know you ought to do,
You'd be so busy you'd forget
The blunders of the folks you've met.

If you were busy being *right,*
You'd find yourself too busy quite
To criticize your brother long,
Because he's busy being wrong.
                    –Author unknown

Forgive

Do you ever stop to think
When you are victim of a wrong,
What a splendid test for self-control
To you has come along?

And angry impulse rises up
Your justice to defend;
You'll give the other back again.
As good as he can send.

If your pride has been severely seared,
Seems nothing more than right
To prove yourself to be a man
And stand right up and fight.

To follow anger's impulse thus
Can only bring regret.
If inclined to carry grudges,
That will bring more trouble yet.

We always have the right of choice
In every act of life,
The right one brings us happiness,
The wrong one, only strife.

The man who willfully does you wrong
With ugly thoughts must live,
But the advantage still is yours–
If you will but forgive.
                    –Author unknown

Forgiving, Tolerance, Mercy, Greed

Bury Your Wrongs

In the very depths of yourself dig a grave. Let it be like some forgotten spot to which no path leads; and there, in the eternal silence, bury the wrongs that you have suffered. Your heart will feel as if a weight has fallen from it, and a divine peace
come to abide with you.
—Charles Wagner

Man's Inhumanity To Man

Many and sharp the numerous ills
   Interwoven with our frame;
More pointed still, we make ourselves
   Regret, remorse and shame;
And man, whose heaven-erected face
   The smiles of love adorn,
Man's inhumanity to man,
Makes countless thousands mourn.
—Robert Burns

On Rising Above The Hurt

My heart was heavy, for its trust had been abused,
Its kindness answered with foul wrong;
So, turning gloomily from my fellow men
One summer Sabbath day, I strolled among
The green mounds of the village burial-place;
Where, pondering how all human love and hate
Find one sad level; and how, soon too late,
Wrong and wrong doer, each with meekened face,
And cold hands folded over a still heart,
Pass the green threshold of our common grave,
Whither all footsteps tend, whence none depart,
Owed for myself, and pitying my race,
Our common sorrow, like a mighty wave,
Swept all my pride away, and trembling, I forgave!
—John Greenleaf Whittier

Forgiving, Tolerance, Mercy, Greed

Let Each Man Learn To Know Himself

Let each man learn to know himself;
To gain this knowledge, let him labor,
Improve those failings in himself
Which he condemns so in his neighbor.
How lenient our own faults we view,
And conscience' voice adroitly smother;
But oh! how harshly we review
The self-same errors in another!

And if you meet an erring one
Whose deeds are blamable or thoughtless,
Consider, ere you cast the stone,
If you yourself be pure and faultless.
Oh! list to that small voice within,
Whose whisperings oft make men confounded,
And trumpet not another's sin,
You'd blush deep if your own were sounded.

And in self-judgment, if you find
Your deeds to others are superior,
To you has Providence been kind,
As you should be to those inferior;
Example sheds a genial ray
Of light which men are apt to borrow;
So, First improve yourself today,
And then improve your friends tomorrow.

—Author unknown

Behold, he who has repented of his sins, the same is forgiven
and I, the Lord, remember them no more.
—D&C 58:42

Forgiving, Tolerance, Mercy, Greed

Evening Prayer

If I have wounded any soul today,
If I have caused one foot to go astray,
If I have walked in my own willful way–
    Good Lord, forgive!

If I have uttered idle words or vain,
If I have turned aside from want or pain,
Lest I myself should suffer through the strain
    Good Lord, forgive!

If I have craved for joys that are not mine,
If I have let my wayward heart repine,
Dwelling on things of earth, not things divine–
    Good Lord, forgive!

If I have been perverse, or hard, or cold,
If I have longed for shelter in Thy fold
When thou hast given me some part to hold–
    Good Lord, forgive!

Forgive the sins I have confessed to Thee,
Forgive the secret sins I do not see,
That which I know not , Father, teach Thou me–
    Help me to live.
                        –C. Maud Battersby

Ye ought to forgive one another; for he that forgiveth not his brother his trespasses standeth condemned before the Lord; for there remaineth in him the greater sin. I, the Lord, will forgive whom I will forgive, but of you it is required to forgive all men. And ye ought to say in your hearts- - let God judge between me and thee, and reward thee according to thy deeds.
    –D&C 64:9-11

Forgiving, Tolerance, Mercy, Greed

A Story To Remember

One night three Arabian Horsemen were riding across the desert. As they crossed the dry bed in a river, out of the darkness a voice called, "Halt!". They obeyed.

The voice told them to dismount, pick up a handful of pebbles, put the pebbles in their pockets, and remount.

The voice then said, "You have done as I commanded. Tomorrow at sun-up you will be both glad and sorry."

Mystified, the horsemen rode on. At sunrise, they reached into their pockets to find a miracle had happened. The pebbles had been transformed into diamonds, rubies, and other precious stones. They remembered the warning. They were both glad and sorry – glad they had taken some and sorry they had not taken more.

–*Author unknown*

In business men talk of service when the real situation is greed for excessive profits.

A young certified public accountant was given the opportunity to make a million dollars in a few months' time by a course of action which in other days would have been regarded as dishonest. He asked his mother for her opinion.

After a few moments' silence she replied, "Jim, you know when I come to wake you in the morning I shake you hard and you don't stir. And I shake you even harder and you give a little moan. And finally I shake you as hard as I can and you open one sleepy eye. I'd hate to come in morning after morning and find you awake!"

He turned the job down and has been sleeping soundly since."

–*Stuart Chase*

Forgiveness, Tolerance, Mercy, Greed

Judge Not

Pray do not find fault with the man
Who limps, or stumbles along the road
Unless you've worn the shoes he wears
Or struggled beneath his load.

    There may be tasks in him that hurt
    Though hidden away from view,
    Or the burden placed on your back
    Might cause you to stumble too.

Unless you've felt the blow
That caused his fall,
Or felt the shame
That only he can know.

    You may be strong, but still the blows
    That were his, if dealt to you
    In selfsame way and selfsame time
    Might cause you to stagger too.

Don't be too harsh with him who sins
Or pelt him with word or stone
Unless you're sure, yea, doubly sure
That you've no sins of your own.

    For you know, perhaps if tempter's voice
    Should whisper soft to you,
    As it did to him that went astray,
    'Twould cause you to falter too.

–Author unknown

Forgiving, Tolerance, Mercy, Greed

Mother's Forgiveness

This beautiful little anecdote illustrates forgiveness and love:

A lad named Sidney, having reached the age of ten, considered he ought to be paid for various little services rendered to his mother in the home. Hearing a conversation concerning certain bills that had to be paid, he conceived the idea of making out a bill for what he had done, and the next morning he quietly laid on his mother's plate the following statement:

Mother owes Sidney: For getting coal six times, 15 cents. For fetching logs of wood lots of times, 15 cents. For going on an errand twice, 10 cents. For being a good boy, 10 cents. Total, 50 cents.

The mother examined the bill, but said nothing. That evening Sidney found it lying on his own plate, with the fifty cents as payment; but accompanying it was another bill, which read as follows:

Sidney owes to mother: For his happy home for ten years – nothing. For nursing him through his illness last year – nothing. For his last new suit of clothes – nothing. For being good to him – nothing.
Total – nothing.

When the lad had looked at this for a moment, his eyes were dim and his lips quivered. Presently he took the fifty cents out of his pocket, and, unable to control his emotion, he rushed to his mother, flung his arms around her neck and exclaimed, 'Mother, dear! I was a mean wretch to give you that bill! Please forgive me and let me do lots of things for you still!' The mother's forgiveness of the debt awakened and increased the boy's love.

–Frank Cox

Forgiving, Tolerance, Mercy, Greed

Forgiveness

Forgiveness is not just a sentimental pardon of one person towards another. It has some prior conditions. One is mercy by the forgiver and the other penitence by the one forgiven. The wrongdoer must be penitent before real forgiveness can take place. Jesus himself said, "If thy brother trespass against thee, rebuke him, and if he repent, forgive him and if he trespass against thee seven times in a day, and seven times in a day turn again to thee, saying, I repent; thou shalt forgive him." (Luke 17:3)

–Author Unknown

What To Forget

If you would increase your happiness and prolong your life, forget your neighbor's faults. Forget all the slander you have ever heard. Forget the temptations. Forget the fault finding, and give a little thought to the cause which provoked it. Forget the peculiarities of your friends, and only remember the good points which make you fond of them.

Forget all personal quarrels or histories you may have heard by accident, and which, if repeated, would seem a thousand times worse than they are. Blot out as far as possible all the disagreeable of life; they will come, but will only grow larger when you remember them, and the constant thought of the acts of meanness or, worse still, malice, will only tend to make you more familiar with them. Obliterate everything disagreeable from yesterday, start out with a clean sheet today, and write upon it for sweet memory's sake only those things which are lovely and lovable.

–Claremont Herald

Forgiving, Tolerance, Mercy, Greed

I'm Going Home

As Tom sat on the train, anxious and apprehensive about what he might soon have to face, the man who sat next to him turned and said, "Son, you seem nervous and worried. Is there anything I can do to help?"

Tom could not hold it back.. He had to tell someone. He had to have a friend to share his deep fear even if it were just a stranger.

"Mister," he said, "I just got out of prison. I won't make excuses, but one thing really haunts me about the mess I've made of my life, and that's the way I broke my parents' hearts. They are old now and have lived in shame for all these years I have been in jail. I do still love them and I want to go home now that I'm out. I know you must think that takes a lot of guts for me to come home after all I have done to them. Well, I feel the same way about it."

Tom paused a few seconds in his story. He looked out at the bleak, bare trees and thought of his tree– the one in his back yard. It was winter now and there was not a thing to be seen on the brittle branches, not even snow.

"I wrote Mom and Dad and asked if I could come home. I wouldn't let them visit me in the crummy jail and so I haven't seen them for a long time. I was just too ashamed to let them come to see me in there."

Tom appreciated the way the man just sat there and listened. He couldn't tell whether he was shocked or sympathetic, but he was listening, and Tom felt he had to talk to someone to take up these last few minutes of agony.

"I told them they did not have to let me come home if they were too ashamed of me. You see, Mister, we live right by the railroad lot. Well, I asked them to tie a ribbon in the ol' tree if they were willing to let me get off." Tom let the alternative go unstated, but his pause spoke it all the louder.

Forgiving, Tolerance, Mercy, Greed

"We're about there now, and – I'm scared to look. I can't blame them if they leave the tree bare. I don't deserve to have a home and the swell Mom and Dad I hurt so deeply."

He started to choke up and looked down to hide his shame. Neither man spoke at all for some time, and then the train began to slow down for the next station; it was Tom's home town.

A few tense moments passed and then the man next to Tom nudged him gently and said, "I think you can look now, Son."
Tom struggled to look up. There was the tree, his tree, marvelously ablaze with hundreds of ribbons – red ones, blue ones, yellow, orange, and green. "I'll see you, Mister," Tom whispered, "I'm going home!"

–Author Unknown

It Will Mend

An ex-governor, in an address that was both kind and witty, said in Philadelphia of the evil of divorce:

"There would be less divorce if there were more forgiveness. We forgive our enemies- - would it be so dreadful to forgive our husbands and our wives?

I have been reading a play by a Frenchman- - *Hervieu's Connaistori* - - I wish we turned out such plays in this country - - and in the last act of this play an old soldier said a profoundly beautiful thing about those husbands and wives who forgive.

"Happiness," he says, "is so precious to some of us that, when it is broken, we stoop and gather up the pieces."

–Author Unknown

Forgiving, Tolerance, Mercy, Greed

Tolerance

Don't condemn a man for what he appears to be; remember you only see the effect, but the cause you may never know.
Isn't it queer that we dislike most in others those unpleasant characteristics we possess ourselves.

–Author Unknown

Forgiving and Forgetting

You who are letting miserable misunderstandings run on from year to year, meaning to clear them up some day: you who are keeping wretched quarrels alive because you cannot quite make up your mind that now is the day to sacrifice your pride and settle them: You who are passing men sullenly upon the street, not speaking to them out of some silly spite:
You who are letting. . . someone's heart ache for a word of appreciation or sympathy, which you mean to give him someday; If you only could know and see and feel, all of a sudden, the time is short, how it would break the spell! How you would go instantly and do the thing which you might never have another chance to do.

–Phillips Brooks

Wrong Doings

The world looks like a multiplication-table or a mathematical equation, which, turn it how you will, balances itself. . . . You cannot do wrong without suffering wrong. . . . A man cannot speak but he judges himself. . . . Every secret is told, every wrong redressed, in silence and certainty. . . . The thief steals from himself. The swindler swindles himself. . . . Men suffer all their life long, under the foolish superstition that they can be cheated. But it is. . . . impossible for a man to be cheated by anyone but himself. . . What will you have? quoth God: pay for it and take it. . . . Thou shalt be paid exactly for what thou hast done, no more, no less.

–Ralph Waldo Emerson

Work, Responsibility, Leisure, Idleness, Debt

Section 19

*Economizing for the purpose of being independent
is one of the soundest indications
of manly character.*
Samuel Smiles

Work, Responsibility, Leisure, Idleness, Debt

It is not enough to be industrious; so are the ants. What are you industrious about?
—Henry David Thoreau

He that is idle shall not eat the bread nor wear the garments of the laborer.
— D&C 42:42

I am glad the eight hour day had not been invented when I was a young man.
—Thomas A. Edison

Without labor nothing prospers.
—Sophocles

A man without a purpose is like a ship without a rudder.
—Thomas Carlyle

Hard work never killed a man, But it sure has scared a lot of them.
—Author unknown

The average person puts only 25% of his energy and ability into his work. The world takes off its hat to those few and far between souls who devote 100%.
—Author unknown

Nothing is so certain as that the evils of idleness can be shaken off by hard work.
—Seneca

The fruit derived from labor is the sweetest of all pleasures.
—Luc de Clapiers Vauvenarjues

Some one's selfish, some one's lazy;
    Is it you?
Some one's sense of right is hazy;
    Is it you?
Some one lives a life of ease,
Doing largely what he please- -
Drifting idly with the breeze;
    Is it you?
—Author unknown

Simplicity is an exact medium between *too little and too much*.
—Sir Joshua Reynolds

Work, Responsibility, Leisure, Idleness, Debt

There is no shame in honorable work.   *–Author unknown*

Whatsoever a man soweth,
That shall he also reap.
–Galatians 6:7

My Little Place

Father, where shall I work today?
   And my love flowed warm and free.
Then He pointed me out a tiny spot
   And said, "Tend that for me."
I answered quickly, "On no, not that!
   Why no one would ever see
No matter how well my work was done,
   Not that little place for me."
And the words He spake, they were not stern,
   He answered me tenderly,
"Ah, little one, search that heart of thine;
   Art thou working for them or me?
Nazareth was a little place,
   And so was Galilee."
–Author Unknown

The Only Way

If the road were easy,
And the burden light,
There'd be no need for courage,
No cause to set things right.
The desert sands are sunny,
Where seldom falls the rain,
But beauty worth the having
Is grown by toil and pain.

No way to pride through pleasure,
No gate to strength through ease,
Strict is the code of honor,
Life gives no cheap degrees.
Knowledge is gained by study,
Patience, the will to work and wait,
For these alone young fellow,
Can make you truly great.
–Author unknown

A victory of success is half won when one gains the habit of work.
–Sarah A. Bolton

There is a difference between sitting before the fire and thinking about doing good, and going out into the cold and doing it.
–Author Unknown

Work, Responsibility, Leisure, Idleness, Debt

He who sits cross-legged with mouth open waiting for roast duck to fly in is going to have a long hunger.
—*Confucian Proverb*

He who complains loudest about the way the ball bounces is very often the one who dropped it.
—*Author unknown*

A healthy person looks upon inaction as the greatest of woes.
—*Author unknown*

Fortune favors the best prepared people. —*Author unknown*

Life is hardly respectable if it has no generous task, no duties or affections that constitute a necessity of existence.
—*Ralph Waldo Emerson*

In idleness there is perpetual despair. —*Thomas Carlyle*

Horse Sense

A horse can't pull while kicking,
 This fact I merely mention,
And he can't kick while pulling,
 Which is my chief contention.

Let's imitate the good old horse
 And lead a life that's fitting;
Just pull an honest load, and then
 There'll be no time for kicking.
—*Author unknown*

I know what happiness is,
for I have done good work.
—*Robert Lewis Stevenson*

The Weary Wisher

I wish I were a little rock,
A sitting on a hill,
A-doing nothing all day long,
But just a sitting still;

I wouldn't eat, I wouldn't sleep,
I wouldn't even wash–
I'd sit and sit a thousand years,
And rest myself, by Gosh!
—*Fredrick P. Latiner*

Work, Responsibility, Leisure, Idleness, Debt

Heights of great men reached and kept were not obtained by sudden flight. They, while their companions slept, toiled upward in the night.   *—Author Unknown*

Each is given a bag of tools,
A shapeless mass, a book of rules.
And each must make, ere life is flown,
A stumbling block or a stepping stone.   *—R.L. Sharpe*

Pray as though everything depends on the Lord. Then get up and go about it as though everything depended upon you.
  —Author unknown

He is not only idle who does nothing, but he is idle who might be better employed.
  —Socrates

The ruin of most men dates from some idle moment.
  —George S. Hillard

With one foot in,
With one foot out,
You can't be in
You can't be out–
Not warm, nor cold
Not square, not round,
More poor than poor
And always bound.
For such a man
Will never know,
Where to begin
Or where to go.
Resolve to begin to live today–
Not tomorrow, but today--
This hour while we have time.
  —Swiss saying

If you want to earn more than you get, you need to be worth more than you are paid.
  —Author Unknown

For what shall it profit a man, if he shall gain the whole world, and lose his own soul   *—Mark 8:36*

The soul is dyed with the color of its leisure thoughts.
  —Author Unknown

Work, Responsibility, Leisure, Idleness, Debt

Getting in debt is getting into a tanglesome net.
—*Benjamin Franklin*

The rich ruleth over the poor, and the borrower is servant to the lender.
—*Proverbs 22:7*

Thems that understands interest receives it, thems that don't pays it.
—*Author Unknown*

The way to be nothing is to do nothing.
—*Nathaniel Howe*

He who owes another does not altogether own himself. Some of his time, his substance, his life, belongs to another until the debt is paid.
—*Author Unknown*

I'm a good believer in luck. The harder I work, the more of it I seem to have.
—*F. L. Emerson*

Faith is to believe what we do not see: and the reward of this faith is to see what we believe.
—*Saint Augustine*

My friend, have you heard of the *town of Yawn*
On the banks of the *River Slow*,
Where the *wait-a-while-flower* blooms so fair,
Where the *sometime-or-other* scents the air and the *soft-go-easy* grow.

It lies in the valley of *what-is-the-use*,
In the province of *Let-'er-slide*,
That tired feeling is native there.
It's the home of the listless *I-don't-care*,
Where the *put-it-offs* abide.
—*Author unknown*

When men are employed, they are best contented, for on the days they worked they were good-natured and cheerful, and with the consciousness of having done a good day's work, they spend the evening Jollily; but on our idle days they were mutinous and quarelsome.
—*Benjamin Franklin*

Work, Responsibility, Leisure, Idleness, Debt

In every variety of human employment there are (those) who do their task perfunctorily, as we say, or just to pass, and as badly as they dare.
 (And there are) those who love work, and love to see it rightly done, who finish their task . . And the state and world is happy, that has the most of such finishers. . . *Work is victory.*   —Ralph Waldo Emerson

Idleness alone is without hope: work earnestly at anytime, you will by degrees learn to work at almost all things. For there is a perennial nobleness and even sacredness in work. . . There is always hope in a man that actually and earnestly works. . . For that is the thing a man is born to.
                              —Thomas Carlyle

Advice To A Young Man

Remember, my son, you have to work. Whether you handle a pick or a pen, a wheelbarrow or a set of books, digging ditches or editing a paper, ringing an auction bell or writing funny things, you must work. If you look around you will see the men who are the most able to live the rest of their days without work are the men who work the hardest. Don't be afraid of killing yourself with overwork. It is beyond your power to do that on the sunny side of thirty. They die sometimes, but it is because they quit work at six p.m. and don't get home until two a.m. It's the interval that kills, my son. The work gives you an appetite for your meals; it lends solidity to your slumbers; it gives you a perfect and grateful appreciation of a holiday.

There are young men who do not work, but the world is not proud of them. It does not know their names, even; it simply speaks of them as "old So-and-So's boys." Nobody likes them; the great busy world doesn't know that they are there. So find out what you want to be and do it, and take off your coat and make a dust in the world. The busier you are the less harm you will be apt to get into, the sweeter your sleep, the brighter and happier your holidays, and the better satisfied will the world be with you.
                              —Robert J. Burdette

Work, Responsibility, Leisure, Idleness, Debt

As A Man Soweth

We must not hope to be mowers
    And to gather the ripe gold ears
Unless we have first been sowers
    And watered the furrows with tears.

It is not just as we take it,
    This mystical world of ours,
Life's field will yield as we make it;
    A harvest of thorns or of flowers.
        –*Johann Wolfgang von Goethe*

I am of the opinion that my life belongs to the whole community, and as long as I live, it is my privilege to do for it whatever I can. I want to be thoroughly used up when I die, for the harder I work, the more I live. I rejoice in life for its own sake. Life is no brief candle to me. It is a sort of splendid torch which I have got hold of for a moment, and I want to make it burn as brightly as possible before handing it on to future generations."
        –*George Bernard Shaw*

How much easier our work would be if we put forth as much effort trying to improve the quality of it as most of us do trying to find excuses for not properly attending to it.
        –*George W. Balli*

Idleness makes all things difficult; but *Industry*, all things easy; And he that *rises late* must trot all day, and shall scarce overtake his business at night; while *Laziness* travels so slow that *Poverty* soon overtake him.
        –*Benjamin Franklin*

Work, Responsibility, Leisure, Idleness, Debt

The Average Man

When it comes to a question of trusting
    Yourself to the risks of the road,
When the thing is the sharing of burdens,
    The lifting the heft of the load,
In the hour of peril or trial,
    In the hour you meet as you can,
You may safely depend on the wisdom
    And skill of the average man.

Tis the average man and no other
    Who does his plain duty each day,
The small thing his was is for doing,
    On the common place bit of the way.
Tis the average man, may God bless him!
    Who pilots us, still in the van,
Over land, over sea, as we travel,
    Just the plain, hardy, average man.

So on through the days of existence,
    All mingling in shadow and shine,
We may count on the every-day hero,
    Whom haply the gods may divine,
But who wears the swart grime of this calling,
    And labors and earns as he can,
And stands at the last with the noblest, –
    The commonplace, average man.
            –Margaret E. Sangster

Thou shalt not be idle; for he that is idle shall not eat the bread nor wear the garments of the laborer.
D & C. 42:42

Work, Responsibility, Leisure, Idleness, Debt

In his book, "Decline and Fall of the Roman Empire", *Edward Gibbon* in 1788 suggested five basic reasons why that great civilization withered and died:
1. The undermining of the dignity and sanctity of the home, which is the basis for human society.
2. Higher and higher taxes: The spending of public money for free bread and circuses for the populace.
3. The mad craze for pleasure: with sports and plays becoming more exciting, more brutal and more immoral.
4. The building of great armaments, when the real enemy was within– The decay or religion, whose leaders lost their touch with life, and their power to guide the people.

Do It Now!

If you've got a job to do, Do it Now!
If it's one you wish were through, Do it Now!
If you're sure the job's your own
Do not hem and haw and groan–Do it Now!

Don't put off a bit of work, Do it Now!
It doesn't pay to shirk, Do it Now!
If you want to fill a place
And be useful to the race
Just get up and take a brace–Do it Now!

Don't linger by the way, Do it Now!
You'll lose if you delay, Do it Now!
If the other fellows wait,
Or postpone until it's late
You hit up a faster gait–Do it Now!
  –Author Unknown

Work, Responsibility, Leisure, Idleness, Debt

It Couldn't Be Done

Somebody said that it couldn't be done,
But he with a chuckle replied
That "maybe it couldn't," but he would be one
Who wouldn't say so till he'd tried.
So he buckled right in with the trace of a grin
On his face. If he worried he hid it.
He started to sing as he tackled the thing
That couldn't be done, and he did it.

Somebody scoffed: "Oh, you'll never do that;
At least no one ever has done it."
But he took off his coat and he took off his hat,
And the first thing we knew he'd begun it.
With a lift of his chin and a bit of a grin,
Without any doubting or quiddit,
He started to sing as he tackled the thing
That couldn't be done, and he did it!

There are thousands to tell you it cannot be done.
There are thousands to prophesy failure;
There are thousands to point out to you, one by one,
The dangers that wait to assail you.
But just buckle in with a bit of a grin,
Just take off your coat and go to it;
Just start to sing as you tackle the thing
That "cannot be done," and you'll do it.

–Edgar A. Guest

Work, Responsibility, Leisure, Idleness, Debt

Work

Don't be afraid of work, it is healthy, physical and mental exercise.
Don't be afraid to push forward, be glad of the chance.
Don't be afraid of failure. Keep on though you may fail a dozen times.
Don't be afraid of difficult undertakings. Be glad of the opportunity to show your mettle.
Don't be afraid of honest competition. It's competition that makes success worthwhile.
Don't be afraid to do more that is required of you.
Don't be afraid that your efforts will not be appreciated.
Don't be afraid to play the game honestly.
  Honesty always wins out.
    –Author unknown

Leisure

What is this life if, full of care,
We have no time to stand and stare.
No time to stand beneath the boughs
And stare as long as sheep or cows.
No time to see, when woods we pass,
Where squirrels hide their nuts in grass.

No time to see, in broad daylight,
Streams full of stars, like skies at night.
No time to turn at Beauty's glance,
And watch her feet, how they can dance.
No time to wait till her mouth can
Enrich that smile her eyes began.

A poor life this is, if full of care,
We have not time to stand and stare.
  –W. H. Davies

Work, Responsibility, Leisure, Idleness, Debt

The Right Sort Of Grit

A neatly dressed country boy with a frank, manly countenance, but with the impress of farm life upon him, walked into the office of the Augusta Chronicle, and said: "Do you happen to know where I can get a job? 'Most any kind of work will do, so it's honorable, and I ain't particular about the pay to start on; provided there's a chance to rise. My name's _____ _____. From Burke county. I see where Augusta is growing. I've come to Augusta to locate and grow up with her."

According to the Chronicle: "Further conversation developed that the young man had just arrived; that he had been engaged in farming all his life, but wanted to strike out in the world for himself, and had determined to come to Augusta and cast his lot. He had just enough to last him for a few days, but he didn't seem to be particularly worried about the future."

The boy added: "I don't know nothing much 'cept farming," he went on to say, "but I am strong and willing and honest, and I haven't got no bad habits, so I thought I might stand about as good a chance as some of the others I've seen come up here from old Burke and make a success. I believe I can learn anything they put me at if I'm given a chance."

Several suggestions were made as to where he might find employment, and he immediately went forth to see what he could find. The Chronicle says: "Within an hour he was back. 'I got turned down in two places, and the other man was out,' he explained. 'But I guess I'll be able to find a job somewhere, don't you?' he asked, still confident. In the meantime the Chronicle had located a job for him. The pay was only a dollar a day, and it was rough work.

The young man was offered the place more to try his mettle than anything else. "I'll take it," he promptly replied. "Guess I can make myself worth more before long, don't you? Anyhow, it's better than walking around looking for work, ain't it?" And he was off to begin his new duties. "I read where a young fellow like me started in with a big concern at 50c cents a day, and is now the general manager," he remarked in parting.

Work, Responsibility, Leisure, Idleness, Debt

The boy has the right spirit. He is not afraid of work, and he is ambitious. If he has capacity he will succeed. He begins with a good capital-youth, health, energy, industry, and a determination to win. It will not be surprising if in a few years he is the head of some large enterprise or industry, and the employer of men of his own age who now scorn to do the work he is doing and who hold themselves the superior of this country boy.

Most of the men of affairs, the leaders in industrial, commercial and professional life in the cities came from the country where they learned the virtue and the value of labor, frugality and thrift. Among the Presidents of railroads and banks and colleges and universities, the commanders of our great battleships, the General of the army, the great lawyers and doctors and surgeons and preachers and merchants and manufacturers and millionaires and authors and thinkers and scientists, a large per cent began life on the farm or in the country, and the foundation of their characters was laid in the simple life which is close to nature.

–*Nashville American*

Work, Responsibility, Leisure, Idleness, Debt

Think what you do when you run in debt; you give to another power over your liberty. If you cannot pay at the time, you will be ashamed to see your creditor; will be in fear when you speak to him; will make poor, pitiful, sneaking excuses, and by degrees come to lose your veracity, and sink into base, downright lying; for the second vice is lying, the first is running in debt. A freeborn man ought not to be ashamed nor afraid to see or speak to any man living, but poverty often deprives a man of all spirit and virtue. It is hard for an empty bag to stand upright.
—Benjamin Franklin

A *bride to be* would do well to ask herself, '*Can my sweetheart manage money? Does he know how to live within his means?*'
A *prospective husband* who is engaged to a young woman who has everything, would do well to *take yet another look and see if she has money management sense.* —Author Unknown

Many who blame the economy for all their financial woes have the wrong target in their sights. The problem, most likely, isn't so much a lack of money as it is the mismanagement of money.
—Author Unknown

For great and low, there is but one test,
Tis that each one shall do his best;
Who works with all the strength he can,
Shall never die in debt to man.
—Author Unknown

Work while it is called today,
for you know not how much you may be hindered tomorrow.
One day is worth two tomorrows;
never leave that till tomorrow which you can do today.
—Benjamin Franklin

Work, Responsibility, Leisure, Idleness, Debt

The Chambered Nautilus

One of the most beautiful creatures of the sea is a small animal known as the Chambered Nautilus. It is a member of an ancient group of animals which are related to the squid and octopus. It is found in the South Pacific and the Indian Ocean. There are only a few species surviving today.

When young it is shaped like a small horn. As the animal develops, the shell grows and begins to take a spiral shape. Within the hollow coil of the shell there is a succession of chambers which are smaller at the center and increases in size with each new chamber. Year after year as the nautilus grows it moves forward building a new chamber. Each new chamber is closed at the rear with mother-of-pearl and is more beautiful and larger than the last. The outer layer of shell is porcelainous and pure ivory in color.

What if the nautilus did not constantly toil to enlarge its chambers? Then it would only be an insignificant animal but because of its beautiful mother-of-pearl luster, it is used in the manufacture of many fancy articles. Like the Nautilus toiling silently year after year to build its lustrous pearl chambers, each of us should be constantly toiling to shape our lives. No one else can make of us that which we are not willing to become.

Watching young people grow is much like watching a sunrise or sunset. As the sunset unfolds, we can not control it...we don't say..now soften the orange just a little on the right hand corner, put a little more purple along the base and use a little more pink in the cloud color. But parents and teachers can be watchful over the youth, offering guidance and love as they unfold, moving forward step by step, year by year as they spiral upward fashioning their own beautiful mother-of-pearl.

This small sea creature was the inspiration for Oliver Wendell Holmes when he wrote the poem Chamber Nautilus in which he called it the Ship of Pearl.
L.W.H.

Work, Responsibility, Leisure, Idleness, Debt

The Chambered Nautilus

This is the ship of pearl, which poets feign,
   Sails the unshadowed main–
   The venturous bark that flings
On the sweet summer wind its purpled wings
In gulfs enchanted, where the Siren sings,
   And coral reefs lie bare,
Where the cold sea-maids rise to sun their
   streaming hair.

Its webs of living gauze no more unfurl;
   Wrecked is the ship of pearl!
   And every chambered cell,.
Where its dim dreaming life was wont to dwell,
As the frail tenant shaped his growing shell,
   Before thee lies revealed,–
Its irised ceiling rent, its sunless crypt unsealed!

Year after year beheld the silent toil
   That spread his lustrous coil;
   Still, as the spiral grew,
He left the past year's dwelling for the new,
Stole with soft step its shining archway through,
   Built up its idle door,
Stretched in his last-found home, and knew the
   old no more.

Thanks for the heavenly message brought by thee,
   Child of the wandering sea,
   Cast from her lap, forlorn!
From thy dead lips a clearer note is born
Than ever Triton blew from wreathed horn!
   While on mine ears it rings,
Through the deep caves of thought I hear a voice
   that sings:

Work, Responsibility, Leisure, Idleness, Debt

Build thee more stately mansions, O my soul,
   As the swift seasons roll!
Leave thy low-vaulted past!
Let each new temple, nobler than the last,
Shut thee from heaven with a dome more vast,
   Till thou at length art free,
Leaving thine outgrown shell by life's unresting
   sea!
                      –*Oliver Wendell Holmes*

In the battle of life it is not the critic who counts; not the man who points out how the strong man stumbled, or where the doer of a deed could have done better. The credit belongs to the man who is actually in the arena; whose face is marked by dust and sweat and blood; who strives valiantly; who errs and comes up short again and again, because there is no effort without error and shortcoming; who does actually strive to do the deeds; who knows the great enthusiasm, the great devotions, spends himself in a worthy cause; who at the best knows in the end the triumph of high achievement; and who at the worst if he fails, at least fails while daring greatly, so that his place shall never be with those cold timid souls who knew neither victory nor defeat.
                      –*Theodore Roosevelt*

There is one advice I must give you. In fact, it is the summary of all advice, and doubtless you have heard it a thousand times; . . . for it is most intensely true, whether you will believe it at present or not: - - namely, That above all things the interest of your whole life depends upon your being diligent, Now while it is called today. . . If you will believe me, you who are young, yours is the golden season of life. . . if you do not sow, or if you sow tares instead of wheat, you cannot expect to reap well afterwards, and you will arrive at little. And in the course of years when you come to look back. . . you will bitterly repent when it is too late.
                      –*Thomas Carlyle*

Work, Responsibility, Leisure, Idleness, Debt

Tomorrow

She is going to be all that a mortal should be, Tomorrow.
No one would be kinder and braver than she, Tomorrow
A friend who was troubled and weary she knew,
Who'd be glad for a lift and who needed it, too
On her she would call and see what she could do, Tomorrow.
And thought of the folks she would fill with delight, Tomorrow.
It was too bad, indeed, she was busy today
And hadn't a minute to stop on her way.
More time she would have to give others, she's say, Tomorrow.
The world would have known her had she ever seen Tomorrow.
But the fact is she died and she faded from view
And all that she left here when living was through,
Was a mountain of things she intended to do, **Tomorrow**.
  –Author unknown

Thank God every morning when you get up that you have something to do that day which must be done whether you like it or not. Being forced to work, and forced to do your best, will breed in you temperance and self control, diligence and strength of will, cheerfulness and content, and a hundred virtues which the idle never know. *–Charles Kingsley*

You cannot help small men by tearing down big men.
You cannot bring down prosperity by discouraging thrift.
You cannot strengthen the weak by weakening the strong.
You cannot lift the wage earner by pulling down the wage payer.
You cannot help the poor man by destroying the rich.
You cannot keep out of trouble by spending more than your income.
You cannot further the brotherhood of man by inciting class hatred.
You cannot establish security on borrowed money.
You cannot build character and courage by taking away man's initiative and independence.
You cannot help men permanently by doing for them what they could and should do for themselves. *–Attributed to Abraham Lincoln*

Work, Responsibility, Leisure, Idleness, Debt

OPEN LETTER TO A TEEN-AGER:

Always we hear the plaintive cry of the teen-agers:
    WHAT CAN WE DO ...?
    WHERE CAN WE GO ...?

The answer is . . . GO HOME!!

Hang the storm windows, paint the woodwork, rake the leaves. Mow the lawn. Shovel the walk. Wash the car. Learn to cook. Scrub some floors. Repair the sink. Build a boat. Get a job. Help the Church. Visit the sick. Assist the poor. Study your lessons. And then when you are through-and not too tired-read a book.

Your parent do not owe you entertainment. Your town does not owe you recreation facilities. The world does NOT owe you a living. You owe the world something. You owe it your time and energy and your talents so that no one will be at war or in poverty, or sick, or lonely again.

In plain simple words: GROW UP; quit being a cry-baby; get out of your dream world, develop a backbone; and start acting like a man or a lady.

I"m a parent. I'm tired of nursing, protecting, helping appealing, begging, excusing, tolerating, denying myself needed comforts for every whim and fancy, just because your selfish ego instead of common sense dominates your personality, and thinking and requests.
                                  JUVENILE COURT

Work, Responsibility, Leisure, Idleness, Debt

The Wise Old Lark

A lark, who had young ones in a field of grain which was almost ripe, was afraid that the reapers would come before her young brood were fledged. So every day when she flew off to look for food, she charged them to take note of what they heard in her absence and to tell her of it when she came home.

One day when she was gone, they heard the owner of the field say to his son that the grain seemed ripe enough to be cut, and told him to go early the next day and ask their friends and neighbors to come and help reap it.

When the old lark came home the little ones quivered and chirped round her and told her what had happened, begging her to take them away as fast as she could. The mother bade them be easy, "For," said she, "if he depends on his friends and his neighbors, I am sure the grain will not be reaped tomorrow."

Next day she went out again and left the same orders as before. The owner came, and waited. The sun grew hot, but nothing was done for not a soul came. "You see," said the owner to his son, "these friends of ours are not to be depended upon; so run off at once to your uncles and cousins, and say I wish them to come early tomorrow morning and help us reap."

This the young ones, in great fright, told also to their mother. "Do not fear, children," said she, "Kindred and relatives are not always very good about helping one another; but keep your ears open and let me know what you hear tomorrow."

The owner came the next day, and , finding his relatives as undependable as his neighbors, said to his son, "Now listen to me. Get two good sickles ready for tomorrow morning, for it seems we must reap the grain by ourselves."

The young ones told this to their mother.

"Then, my dears," said she, "it is time for us to go; for when a man undertakes to do his work himself, it is not so likely that he will be disappointed." She took away her young ones at once, and the grain was reaped the next day by the old man and his son.

Depend upon yourself alone!

—Author Unknown

Work, Responsibility, Leisure, Idleness, Debt

Work

How do you tackle your work each day?
   Are you scared of the job you find?
Do you grapple the task that comes your way
   With a confident, easy mind?
Do you stand right up to the work ahead
   Or fearfully pause to view it?
Do you start to toil with a sense of dread
   Or feel that you're going to do it?

        You can do as much as you think you can
           But you'll never accomplish more;
        If you're afraid of yourself, young man,
           There's little for you in store.
        For failure comes from the inside first,
           It's there if we only knew it,
        And you can win, though you face the worst,
           If your feel that you're going to do it.

Success! It's found in the soul of you,
   And not in the realm of luck!
The world will furnish the work to do,
   But you must provide the pluck.
You can do whatever you think you can,
   It's all in the way you view it.
It's all in the start that you make, young man:
   You must feel that you're going to do it.
                –*Edgar A. Guest*

Work, Responsibility, Leisure, Idleness, Debt

Nothing is more unworthy of a wise man . . . than to have allowed more time for trifling and useless things than they deserve.

–Plato

When we look into the long avenue of the future, and see the good there is for each of us to do, we realize after all what a beautiful thing it is to work and to live and be happy.

–Robert Lewis Stevenson

Procrastination is the art of keeping up with yesterday.

–Don Marquis

What would be the use of immortality to a person who cannot use well a half hour. Five minutes of today are worth as much to me as five minutes in the next millennium.

–Ralph Waldo Emerson

This life is the time for men to prepare to meet God; yea, behold the day of this life is the day for men to perform their labors.

–Alma 34:32

Always Finish

If a task is once begun,
Never leave it till lit's done.
Be th labor great or small,
Do it well or not at all.
–Author Unknown

Work, Responsibility, Leisure, Idleness, Debt

My Work

If you have work, do it well.

He was right who said:
"Let me but do my work
from day to day,
In field or forest, at the desk or loom;
In roaring market place or tranquil room;
Let me but find it in my heart to say,
when vagrant wishes beckon me astray,
'This is my work; my blessing, not my doom.
Of all who live, I am the one by whom
This work can best be done in the right way.'
Then shall I see it not too great nor small,
To suit my spirit and to prove my powers;
Then shall I cheerful greet the laboring hours,
And cheerful turn when the long shadows fall
At eventide, to play and love and rest,
Because I know for me my work is best."
—*Author Unknown*

Work, Responsibility, Leisure, Idleness, Debt

Managing Money

Anyone who has bogged down in quicksand will tell you it's easier to stay out of it than get out of it. The same applies to debt.
–Author Unknown

When Prosperity comes, do not use all of it.
–Confucious

Ah, all things come to those who wait,
(I say these words to make me glad),
But something answers soft and sad,
They come, but often come too late.
–Mary Singleton

To men prepared, Delay is always hurtful.
–Dante

The person rowing the boat seldom has time to rock it.
–Author Unknown

He who cuts his own firewood is twice warmed.
–Author Unknown

Smiles, Laughter, Hugs, Humor

Section 20

*Laugh, and the world laughs with you;
Weep, and you weep alone.*
Ella Wheeler Wilcox

Smiles, Laughter, Hugs, Humor

Smile

If you chance to meet a frown,
  Do not let it stay.
  Quickly turn it upside down
  And smile the frown away.

No one likes a frowning face
  Change it for a smile.
Make the world a better place
  By Smiling all the while.
  –*Daniel Taylor*

If I knew you and you knew me,
If both of us could clearly see,
And with an inner sight divine
The meaning of your heart and mine.

I'm sure that we would differ less,
and clasp our hands in friendliness,
  Our thoughts would pleasantly agree
If I knew you and you knew me.
  –*Nixon Waterman*

⁕⁘⁕

God gave all people in every nation the ability to smile and laugh in the same language.
  –*Author unknown*

A smile is the same in any language. –*Author Unknown*

Infection

A baby smiled in its mother's face;
The mother caught it, and gave it then
To the baby's father--serious case--
Who carried it out to the other men;
And every one went straight away
Scattering sunshine thro' the day.
  –*Lois de Louk*

A smile is a curve that can set a lot of things straight.
  –*Author unknown*

Actions speak louder than words,
And a smile says, "I like you.
You make me happy.
I am glad to see you."
Author unknown

Smiles, Laughter, Hugs, Humor

When you meet a person without a smile, give him one of yours.
—Author unknown

They may not need me, but they might.
I'll try to keep my head in sight.
A smile as small as mine might be
Precisely their necessity.
—Emily Dickinson

A good laugh is sunshine in a house.
—William M. Thackeray

A smile increases your face value.
—Author unknown

Smile

The smile that you gave to me that day
When I was lone and sad,
Did much to lift my drooping soul,
And make my heart feel glad.

Since then, I give away my smiles
To those upon life's way,
For they may need them just as much,
As I did yours, that day.
—Author unknown

Have you tried out your smile today?
To light your steps along the way?
It's mirrored in each face you meet
On byways, path and city street.

Have you tried out your smile today?
A smile that's sunny, bright and gay,
That helps to lift somebody's grief,
And brings to pain some small relief?

Have you tried out your smile today?
If not, you should not delay.
You'll find you heart is gladdened, too,
When someone else smiles back at you.
—Verna Young

Smiles, Laughter, Hugs, Humor

Smile

It's easy enough to be pleasant
When life flows like a song;
But the man worthwhile
Is the man who can smile
When everything goes dead wrong.
For the test of the heart is trouble
And it always comes with the years
And the smile that is worth the praises of earth
Is the smile that shines through tears.

It's easy enough to be virtuous
When nothing tempts you to stray;
When without or within no voice of sin
Is luring your soul away.
But it's only a negative virtue
Until it is tried by fire;
And the life that is worth the honor of earth
Is the life that resists desire.

By the cynic, the sad, the fallen,
Who had no strength of the strife;
The world's highway is cumbered today
They make up the item of life.
But the virtue that conquers passion;
And sorrow that hides in a smile;
It is these that are worth the homage of earth
For we find them but once in a while.

–Ella Wheeler Wilcox

Smiles, Laughter, Hugs, Humor

Keep Smiling

My father smiled this morning when
He came downstairs, you see,
At mother and, when he smiled, then
She turned and smiled at me;
And when she smiled at me I went
And smiled at Mary Ann
Out in the kitchen; and she lent
It to the baker's man.

So then he smiled at someone whom
He saw when going by,
Who also smiled, and ere he knew,
Had twinkles in his eye;
So he went to his office then,
And smiled right at his clerk,
Who put some more ink on his pen,
And smiled back from his work.

And when this clerk went home he smiled
Right at his wife; and she
Smiled over at his little child,
As happy as could be;
And then the little girlie took
The smile to school; and, when
She smiled at teacher from her book,
The teacher smiled back again.

And then the teacher passed on one
To little Jim McBride,
Who couldn't get his lessons done
No matter how he tried;
And Jimmy took it home, and told
How teacher smiled at him
When he was tired, and didn't scold,
But said, "Don't worry, Jim."

Smiles, Laughter, Hugs, Humor

And when I happened to be there
That very night to play,
Jim's mother had a smile to spare,
Which came across my way;
And then I took it for a while
Back home, and Mother said:
"Here is that very selfsame smile
Come back with us to bed."
—*Author unknown*

Hugs

It's wondrous what a hug can do,
A hug can cheer you when you're blue.
A hug can say, "I love you so,"
Or, "Gee, I hate to see you go."
A hug is, "Welcome back again,"
And, "Great to see you! Where've you been?"
A hug can soothe a small child's pain
And bring a rainbow after rain.

The hug! There's just no doubt about it,
We scarcely could survive without it!
A hug delights, and warms, and charms,
It must be why God gave us arms.
Hugs are great for fathers and mothers,
Sweet for sisters, swell for brothers.
And chances are your favorite aunts
Love them more than potted plants.

Kittens crave them, puppies love them.
Heads of state are not above them.
A hug can break the language barrier
And make your travels so much merrier.
No need to fret about your store of 'em;
The more you give the more there's of 'em.
So stretch those arms without delay and
Give Someone A Hug Today!!
—*Author unknown*

Smiles, Laughter, Hugs, Humor

L o v e C a k e

1. Take two heaping measures of *affection* and mix together with *devotion*.

2. Sweeten with *tenderness*

3. Sprinkle in some *laughter* and fun according to taste.

4. Flavor with a cup of *happiness*

an ounce of *understanding*

A bushel of *tolerance* and *forgiveness*.

5. Stir the batter well; even all through, till there is no room for discord nor regrets.

6. Bake in a warm oven of *respect* and *companionship* for as long as it takes.

7. Serve on any occasion, any season, any place, any time.

8. Avoid serving with tongue or cold shoulder.
–Author Unknown

Smiles, Laughter, Hugs, Humor

Three Rolls and a Pretzel

One day a peasant bought himself a large roll and ate it. He was still very hungry, so he bought another roll and ate it. This still did not satisfy his hunger so he bought a third roll and ate it. Since the three rolls failed to satisfy his hunger, he decided to buy some pretzels. After eating only one pretzel his hunger was satisfied.

Throwing his hands above his head, he cried out, "What a fool I am! I wasted all those rolls when I ought to have eaten just one pretzel in the first place!"

—*Leo Tolstoy*

Oh!

Oh, what would people do
Without the little Oh?
For everyone says it
Wherever they may go.
When people bump their noses,
Or even stub a toe,
How very much they'd suffer
If they couldn't cry out "Oh!"

It's Oh! When I am happy
And Oh my! When I'm sad,
And Oh dear me! When study
Makes me so awful mad.

When I go to the dentist
I sound frightful, Oh!
And then when I am asleep
There is the gaping O-H!

—*Author Unknown*

Smiles, Laughter, Hugs, Humor

Ma's Tools

At home it seems to be the rule
Pa never has "the proper tool"
Or knack to fix things. For the stunt
That stumps ma, though, you'll have to hunt.

The *caster* on the table leg
Fell out. Pa said a wooden peg
Would fix it up. But ma *kep 'mum*
An' fixed it with a *wad of gum*.

We could scarce open our front door,
it stuck so tight. An' pa, he swore
He'd "buy a *plane"* as big as life–
Ma fixed it with the *carving* knife.

The *bureau drawer* got *stuck* one day,
An' push or pull, 'twas there to stay.
Says pa, "Some day 'twill *shrink*, I hope."
Ma *fixed* it with a *piece* of soap.

The *window-shade* got out of *whack*,
'Twould not pull down, nor yet roll back.
Pa says, "No one can fix that thing."
Ma fixed it with a *piece of string*.

I broke the *stove-door hinge* one day.
('Twas cracked before, though, anyway.)
Pa said we'd put a new door in.
Ma grabbed her hair an' got a pin.

The *bath-tub drain* got all clogged up.
Pa bailed the tub out with a cup—
He had a dreadful, helpless look.
Ma cleaned it with a crochet-hook.

Smiles, Laughter, Hugs, Humor

One day our *old clock* wouldn't start.
Pa said he'd take it all apart
Some day an' fix the ol' machine.
Ma soused the works in gasoline.

The garden-gate *latch* broke one day,
Cows ate our sw**e**et *corn* up. An', say,
Pa scolded like a house afire!
Ma fixed the latch up with hay wire.

So when my things get out of fix
Do I ask pa to mend 'em?   Nix.
But ma just grabs what's near *at* hand
An' togs things up to *beat* the band.
   –Author Unknown

The Bible

I found an old dusty book high
  on the shelf, "Just look!"
"Why that's the Bible , Dear,
Be careful that's God's Book."

"God's book!" the child exclaimed.
"Then mother, before we loose it,
Don't you think we'd better
Send it back to God–
For you know we never use it!"
   –Author Unknown

Smiles, Laughter, Hugs, Humor

Two Little Kittens

Two little kittens, one stormy night
Began to quarrel and then to fight;
One had a mouse
the other had none,
And that was the way the quarrel begun.

"*I'll have that mouse,*" said the biggest cat
"*You'll* have *that mouse*, we'll see about that."
"*I will have that mouse,*" said the eldest son.
"*You shan't have that mouse,*" said the little one.

I told you before
'twas a stormy night
When these two little kittens began to fight;
The old woman seized her sweeping-broom
And swept the two kittens
right out of the room.

The ground was covered with frost and snow,
And the two little kittens
had nowhere to go.
So they laid them down on the mat at the door,
While the old woman
finished sweeping the floor.

Then they both crept in, as quiet as mice;
All wet with snow
and cold as ice;
For they found it was better, that stormy night,
To lie down and sleep, than to quarrel and fight.
—*Author Unknown*

Smiles, Laughter, Hugs Humor

Playing Hookey

I remember when in boyhood,
Just a step advanced from toyhood,
When in through the schoolroom window
floated sweet the wild birds' call,
I would close my desk at dinner
Like a hardened little sinner,
And the after-nooning found me *playing hookey from it all.*

What to us the far-off sorrow
Of the whipping on the morrow,
For the day seemed all the future'twas a hundred hours long,
And each hour we were enjoying
By the wood and pool-just boying,
While the wild birds caught our laughing *tones*
And wove them into song.

And today a robin twitterd
Through the window and my littered
desk became the ink-bespattered one
my school days used to know,
When the voice of summer crying
And some voice in me replying
To its very note and echo –
and some yearning bade me go.

But the sterner duty fetters
Me to these unanswered letters
While through half-opened shutters
the wild birds cry and call,
And I'm wishing, wishing, wishing,
I might steal off somewhere, fishing,
Lock up every care and worry–
Just play hookey from it all .
    –*Author Unknown*

Smiles, Laughter, Hugs, Humor

A Monkey's Viewpoint

Three monkeys dining in a cocoanut tree
Were discussing something they thought shouldn't be.
Said one to the others, "Now, listen you two–
Here monkeys, is something that cannot be true
That humans descended from our noble race!
Why, it's a shock–a terrible disgrace!
Whoever heard of a monkey
deserting his wife;
Leaving a baby to starve;
maybe ruin its life?

"And have you ever known
of a mother monk
To leave her darling
with strangers to bunk?
Human babies are handed
from one to another
And some scarcely
know the love
of a mother."
–*Author Unknown*

Mr. Meant-To has a comrade,
And his name is Didn't-Do;
Have you ever chanced to meet them?
Did they ever call on you?

These two fellows live together
In the house of Never-Win,
And I'm told that it is haunted
By th ghost of Might-Have-Been.
–*Author Unknown*

Smiles, Laughter, Hugs, Humor

The Blind Men And The Elephant

It was six men of Indostan to learning much inclined,
Who went to see the elephant (though all of them were blind),
That each by observation might satisfy his mind,

The *First* approached the elephant, and happening to fall
Against his *broad* and *sturdy side*, at once began to bawl:
"God bless me! But the elephant is *nothing but a wall!*"

The *Second*, feeling of the *tusk*, cried:"Ho what have we here
So very round and smooth and sharp? "To me 'tis mighty clear
This wonder of an elephant is *very like a spear!*"

The *Third* approached the animal, and happening to take
The squirming *trunk* within his hands, thus boldly up and spake:
"I see," quoth he, "the elephant is *very like a snake!*"

The *Fourth* reached out his eager hand, and felt about the *knee*;
"What most this wonderous beast is like is mighty plain,"quoth he;
"tis clear enough the elephant is *very like a tree.*"

The *Fifth*, who chanced to touch the *ear*, said: "E'en the blindest man
Can tell what this resembles most; deny the fact who can,
This marvel of an elephant is *very like a fan!*"

The *Sixth* no sooner had begun about the beast to grope,
Than seizing on the swinging *tail* that fell within his scope,
"I see," quoth he, "the elephant is *very like a rope!*"

And so these men of Indostan disputed loud and long,
Each in his own opinion exceeding stiff and strong,
Though each was partly in the right, and all were in the wrong!

So, oft in theologic wars the disputants I ween,
Of what each other mean flail on in utter ignorance
And prate about *an elephant not one of them has seen*!

–John Godfrey Saxe

Smiles, Laughter, Hugs, Humor

The Under Dog

I know that this world—that the great big world—
　　From the peasant up to the king,
　Has a different tale from the tale I tell,
　　And a different song to sing.

　But for me and I care not a single fig
　　If they say I am wrong or I'm right;
　I shall always go in for the weaker dog,
　　The under dog in the fight.

I know that the world—that the great big world—
　　Will never a moment stop
　To see which dog may be in fault,
　But will shout for the dog on the top.

　But for me—I never shall pause to ask
　　Which dog may be in the right;
　For my heart will beat, while it beats at all.
　　For the under dog in the fight.

　Perchance what I've said were better not said,
　　Or 'twere better I said it incog;
But with heart and with glass filled chock to the brim,
　　Here is luck to the bottom dog.
　　　—Author Unknown

Smiles, Laughter, Hugs, Humor

Family Financiering

"They tell me you work for a dollar a day;
How is it you clothe your six boys on such pay?

"I know you will think it conceited and queer,
But I do it because I'm a good financier.

"There's Pete, John, Jim and Joe and William and Ned,
A half-dozen boys to be clothed up and fed.

"And I buy for them all good plain victuals to eat,
And clothing–I only buy clothing for Pete.

"When Pete's clothes are too small for him to go on,
My wife makes 'em over and gives them to John.

"When John who is ten, they have grown out of date,
She just makes 'em over for Jim, who is eight.

"When for Jim they become too ragged to fix,
She just makes 'em over for Joe, who is six.

"And when little Joseph can't wear them no more,
She just makes 'em over for Bill, who is four.

"And when for young Bill they no longer will do,
She just makes 'em over for Ned, who is two.

"So you see, if I get enough clothing for Pete
The family is furnished with clothing complete."
"But when Ned gets through with the clothing and when
He has thrown it aside, what do you do with it then?"
"Why, once more we go around the circle complete,
And begin to use it for patches for Pete."

–Author Unknown

Smiles, Laughter, Hugs, Humor

Dad's Old Breeches

When dad has worn his trousers out,
They pass to brother John.
Then mother trims them round about,
And William puts them on.

When William's legs too long have grown,
The trousers fail to hide 'em,
So Walter claims them for his own
And stows himself inside 'em.

Next Sam's fat legs they close invest,
And, when they won't stretch tighter,
They're turned and shortened,
washed and pressed
And fixed on me–the writer.

Ma works them into rugs and caps
When I have burst the stitches.
As doomsday we shall see (perhaps)
That last of dad's old breeches.
        –Author Unknown

The Hardship Of Accounting

Never ask of money spent,
Where the spender thinks it went.
Nobody was ever meant
To remember or invent
What he did with every cent
        –Author Unknown

Smiles, Laughter, Hugs, Humor

The Value Of A Smile

It cost nothing, but creates much.
It enriches those who receive,
Without impoverishing those who give.
It happens in a flash, and the memory of it
Sometimes lasts forever.

None are so rich
They can get along without it,
And none are so poor
But are richer for its benefits.
It creates happiness in the home,
Fosters good will in a business,
And is the countersign of friends.

It is rest to the weary,
Daylight to the discouraged,
Sunshine to the sad,
And nature's best antidote for trouble.

Yet it cannot be bought, begged,
Borrowed, or stolen,
For it is something that is
No earthly good to anybody
Till it is given away!

For nobody needs a smile
So much as those
Who have none left to give!
So practice smiling.
　　–*Author unknown*

Smiles, Laughter, Hugs, Humor

Why Laugh?

1. Laughter reduces your stress.
2. Laughter makes others wonder what you are up to.
3. Laughter makes people want to be around you.
4. Laughter adds life to your years.
5. Laughter adds years to your life.
1. Laughter helps put your wrinkles in the right place.
7. Laughter reduces your tension.
8. Laughter stimulates your immune system.
9. Laughter makes life's problems easier to bear.
10. Laughter makes you feel good all over.
11. Laughter makes you more alert.
12. Laughter eases your pain.
13. Laughter makes other people feel better.
14. Laughter brings tears which cleanse the eyes.
15. Laughter makes you forget about your problems for a while.
16. Laughter puts a twinkle in your eye.
17. Laughter puts a smile on your face.
18. Laughter puts a smile on someone else's face.
19. Laughter helps you take life a bit less seriously.
20. Laughter will reduce the time you need in therapy.
21. Laughter is contagious.
22. Laughter is free.

–Author unknown

There are three kinds of people in all organizations. There are the rowboat people, the sail boat people and the steam boat people.
The rowboat always needs to be pushed or shoved along.
The sailboat people move along when a favorable wind is blowing. But the steamboat moves along continuously, through calm or storm. They are masters of themselves and their surroundings.
In what class are you?

–Author Unknown

Smiles, Laughter, Hugs, Humor

Let Us Smile

The thing that goes the fartherest towards making life worth while
That cost the least and does the most, is just a pleasant smile,
The smile that bubbles from the heart that loves its fellowmen
Will drive away the cloud of gloom and coax the sun again,
It's full of worth and goodness too, with manly kindness blent–
It's worth a million dollars, and doesn't cost a cent.

There is no room for sadness when we see a cheery smile;
It always has the same good look–it's never out of style–
It nerves us on to try again when failure makes us blue;
The dimples of encouragement are good for me and you.
It pays a higher interest, for it is merely lent–
It's worth a million dollars, and doesn't cost a cent.

A smile comes very easy–you can wrinkle up with cheer
A hundred times before you can squeeze out a soggy tear,
It ripples out, moreover, to the heart-strings that will tug,
And always leaves an echo that is very like a hug.
So, smile away. Folks understand what by a smile is meant
It's worth a million dollars, and doesn't cost a cent.
–W. D. Nesbitt

I love the man that can smile in trouble, that can gather strength from distress, and grow brave by reflection. It is the business of little minds to shrink, but he whose conscience approves his conduct, will pursue his principles unto death.
–Thomas Paine

A young boy came home from Sunday School and his mother ask him what he had learned. He remarked, "A man came with a quilt." The mother was at a loss as to what he meant, so she called his teacher and the teacher said: "The lesson was: The Comforter Cometh."
–Author Unknown

Smiles, Laughter, Hugs, Humor

A Smile Says A Lot

A smile's a warm expression that has the nicest way of telling all the special thoughts our hearts would like to say.

It says, "I'm glad I'm friends with you." It says, "I think you're grand." And when you want to be alone, it says, "I understand."

It happens when you hear good news 'bout someone nice you know. It happens when you're all dressed up and have someplace nice to go.

There really isn't very much a sunny smile can't do. It says, "Thank you", when a friend of yours does something just for you.

And when you do something thoughtful, as you've often done for me, the smile that says "You're welcome," is as warm as it can be!

And sometimes friends disagree about silly stuff–and then–the smile that says, "I'm sorry," will patch things up again!

A smile's a happy little curve that has a magic way of straightening out and brightening up even a cloudy day.

Some smiles are sweet and bashful; some are big and wide. But they always say the same old thing–you're feeling good inside!

And when a smile gets extra large from some extra sun-filled joys– then we call it "laughter"–A smile making noise!!

But sometimes when we're busy, we forget the way a smile can make everything we're doing ever more worthwhile.

–*Author unknown*

Smiles, Laughter, Hugs, Humor

Harry's Lecture

Children should be seen and not heard, at least so my mother often tells me. But today the children are to be heard as well as seen. Just as I stepped up here to speak my piece, my teacher whispered, "Now, Harry, Speak very loud." And that is what I am trying to do. Can you hear me? I am going to give a little lecture to the boys, and I want to be heard.

Never mind what it is about. You will find that out before I am half way through.

And now for my *firstly*: Do you want to know how to be happy all day, boys? Let me tell you. When you get up in the morning, don't forget to slip on your "good-natured coat" before you go down the stairs. You all have one, haven't you? And then you don't care if everybody is done with breakfast and the buckwheats are cold.

Secondly. When everything goes wrong at home, at school, or in the street, and you think you have enough trouble to put any boy in a bad humor, then (slowly) you may depend upon it, boys, some one is trying to rob you of your "good-natured coat." But don't let it go. Hold on to it with a tight grip, and when you feel it settling firmly back into its place, Oh, MY! How jolly you will feel.

Thirdly. I have found out, boys, that it pays to wear this coat. And the beauty of it is, you can wear it in all kinds of weather. It is just as useful on a stormy day as on a fair, sunny one. Indeed, it often makes a dull, cloudy day seem very bright and golden.

And now *lastly*: Be good-natured, always. Put cross people in a good humor by being pleasant and cheerful. Give a smile for a frown, a gentle word for a cross one; and this you can do if you are careful to put on your "good-natured coat" as soon as you arise in the morning, and to wear it all day and in all kinds of weather.

–L.F. Rook

Smiles, Laughter, Hugs, Humor

If You Can Smile

If you can smile when things go wrong
And say, "It doesn't matter,"
If you can laugh off care and woe
And trouble makes you fatter;

If you can keep a happy face
When all around are blue–
Then have your head examined, Bud,
There's something wrong with you.

For one thing I've arrived at:
There are no "ands" or "buts";
The guy that's grinning all the time
Must be completely nuts.
–*Author unknown*

Zig Zag Children

I know a little zigzag boy
Who goes this way and that.
He never knows just where he puts
His coat or shoes or hat.

I know a little zigzag girl
Who flutters here and there.
She never knows just where to find
Her brush to fix her hair.

If you are not a zigzag child
You'll have no cause to say,
That you forgot for you will know
Where things are put away.
–*Author Unknown*

Smiles, Laughter, Hugs, Humor

Why People Go To Church

Some go to church just for a walk;
Some go to stare and laugh and talk.
Some go there to meet a friend;
Some their idle time to spend.

      Some for general observation;
      Some for private speculation.
      Some go there to use their eyes,
      The latest fashions to criticize.

Some to scan a dress or bonnet,
Some to price the doodads on it.
Some to gossip, false and true,
Safely hid in the shelt'ring pew.

      Some because it's thought genteel,
      Some to show their pious zeal.
      Some to show how sweet they sing,
      Some how loud their voices ring.

Some the preacher go to hear,
His style and voice to praise or jeer.
Some forgiveness to implore,
Some their sins to varnish o'er.

      Some to sit and doze and nod,
      But very few to Worship God.
                –*Author Unknown*

Smiles, Laughter, Hugs, Humor

A Sunday School teacher asked her children to draw a picture of some incident in the Bible. One little girl drew a picture of an airplane with four passengers. When she showed it to her teacher, the teacher remarked: "I'm sure this is a nice plane and I imagine it can travel very fast, but what has it got to do with the Bible.
Enthusiastically, the little girl said: "Well, this is the flight of Mary and Joseph and Baby Jesus into Egypt."
"Yes, " said the teacher, "But who is the fourth person?"
"Oh that's Pontius the pilot."   *–Author Unknown*

The Two Bills

Two bills were waiting in the bank for their turn to go out into the world. One was a little bill, only one dollar; the other was a big bill, a thousand-dollar bill.

While lying there, side-by-side, they fell a-talking about their usefulness. The dollar bill murmured:

"Ah, if I were as big as you what good I would do! I could move in such high places, and people would be so careful of me wherever I should go! All would admire me, and want to take me home with them, but, small as I am, what good can I do? Nobody cares much for me. I am too little to be of any use."

"Ah, yes! That is so," said the thousand-dollar bill; and it haughtily gathered up its well-trimmed edges, that were lying next the little bill, in conscious superiority. "That is so," it repeated. "If you were as great as I am–a thousand times bigger than you are–then you might hope to do some good in the world." And its face smiled a wrinkle of contempt for the little dollar bill.

Smiles, Laughter, Hugs, Humor

"Just then the cashier came, took the little, murmuring bill, and kindly gave it to a poor widow.

"God bless you!" she cried, as with a smiling face she received it. "My dear, hungry children can now have some bread."

A thrill of joy ran through the little bill as it was folded up in the widow's hand, and it whispered: "I may do some good, even if I am small." And when it saw the bright faces of her fatherless children, it was very glad that it could do a little good.

Then the little dollar bill began its journey of usefulness. It went first to the baker's for bread, then to the miller's, then to the farmer's, then to the laborer's, then to the doctor's, then to the minister's and wherever it went it gave pleasure, adding something to their comfort and joy. At last, after a long, long pilgrimage of usefulness among every sort of people, it came back to the bank again, crumpled, defaced, ragged, softened, by its daily use.

Seeing the thousand-dollar bill lying there with scarcely a wrinkle or a fingermark upon it, it exclaimed: "Pray, sir, and what has been your mission of usefulness?" The big bill sadly replied: "I have been from safe to safe, among the rich, where few could see, me, and they were afraid to let me go out far, lest I should be lost. Few, indeed are they whom I have made happy by my mission."

The little dollar bill said, "It is better to be small and go among the multitudes doing good, than to be so great as to be imprisoned in the safes of the few." And it rested satisfied with its lot.

(Moral.–*The doing well of little every-day duties makes one the most useful and happy.*)

–*Author Unknown*

INDEX
BY

Authors known

Authors unknown
and
First line of text
(in order of appearance)

Section 11 **Authors**: Mother and Father Influence

George. Washington: I attribute all my success in life
Abe Lincoln: All that I am or hope to be
Thomas Edison: MY mother was the making of me

Woodrow Wilson: asked that the American flag be put out on
Joy Allison: Which Loved Best
New Orleans Picayune: Send Them To Bead With A Kiss

Naomi Johnstone: To My Mother
Alice Hawthorne: What Is Home Without A Mother
Joaquin Miller: The Bravest Battle

Temple Bailey: A Little Parable for Mothers
Hearthstone: True Words Well Said
Stephen B. Leaycock: How We kept Mother's Birthday

George Herbert: One father is worth more than a hundred
Edgar A. Guest: Only A Dad: with a tired face
Naomi Johnstone: Dad: These memories are of our dad

Edgar A. Guest: We've never seen the Father here,
Calvin R. Worthington: My Father's Hands
Edgar A. Guest: His Example..There are little eyes upon you
LWH: The Making of a Lasting Marriage

Section 11 **Unknown**   Mother and Father Influence

Mother's face: Three little boys talked together
My mother gave to me everything money can not buy.
Only One Mother: Hundreds of stars in the pretty sky

When Mother's There: When mothers anywhere around
The mother in her office
A Prayer: Father I thank Thee for my Mother

What Matters: My mother says, she doesn't care about the
Mother's Boys: Yes, I know there are stains on my carpet
Memory: I stood and watched him playing

Somebody's Mother: The woman was old, and ragged and
I wish I had the Power to write
When you thought I wasn't looking

A Dad's Great Job: I may never be as clever
That Boy: He wants to be like his dad!
To My Grown -up Son" My hands were busy through the day

Father's Footsteps: A father and his tiny son
What Makes a Dad? God took the strength of a mountain
Why God Made Fathers: God knew that children all would

Please Daddy Let's Go: A little girl with shining eyes
Father and Sons: Last evening about five o'clock
If the best in boys were found in more men
A Father's Prayer

Section 12 **Known** Authors: Freedom, Justice, Liberty, Patriotism

Patrick Henry: Is life so dear
Wm. Penn: If men be good
Edmund Burke: What is liberty
Henry Ward Beecher There is no liberty
Andrew Jackson: No free government can stand
George Washington: Labour to keep alive in your breast
Abraham Lincoln: The best thing about the future is
F.D. Roosevelt:: Ideas are not limited
Horace: Who then is free?
Franklin D. Roosevelt: The test of our progress

Benjamin Franklin We must all hang together
Abraham Lincoln: Those who deny freedom to other
Sir Walter Scott: True patriotism is a matter of deeds
Abraham Lincoln: A house divided
John F. Kennedy: Let every nation know,
Charles Kingsley: There are two freedoms
Alexis de Tocqueville: America is great because America is good.
Abraham Lincoln: This is a world of compensation
Franklin D. Roosevelt: Remember always that all of us
Wm. Somerset Maughan: There are two good things in life

Daniel Webster: No man can suffer too much
Daniel Webster: If we work upon marble, it will perish
Lloyd George: In his life he was a great American
William Penn: Men must be governed by God or they will be ruled
William C. Clegg: Know this that every soul is free
Emma Lazarus: Give me you tired, your poor
Theodore Parker: A democracy that is a government
Henry David Thoreau The fate of the country
James Russell Lowell: They are slaves who fear to speak
George Washington: Almighty God, we make our earnest prayer

(Continued)

William T. Page: I believe in the United States of America
Abraham Lincoln: We have been the recipients
Sir Walter Scott: Breathes there the man
Frank K. Lane (1937: Makers of the Flag
Abraham Lincoln: With malice toward none
Thomas Jefferson: God who gave us life
Daniel Webster: If we and our posterity
J. William Jones: The Responsive Chord
Portland Me. A Beautiful Allegory
Abraham Lincoln: Dear Madam

James Bryce: Patriotism consists not in waving the flag
New England Adage: Faith, Hope and Charity
Thomas Jefferson: The Bible is the source of liberty
Sherwood Eddy: True patriotism is a matter of deeds
Henry Van Dyke: So it's home again and home again
James Russell Lowell: Once to every man and nation comes the momen
Walt Whitman: O, Captain! My Captain!
Francis Brett Young: What were you carrying, Pilgrims,.
Theodore Roosevelt: To The Boys of America
Thomas Paine: When it shall be said

Section 12: **UnKnown** Freedom, Justice, Liberty, Patriotism

None

Section 13 **Authors**: Friendship, Happiness, Kindness, Courtesy

Joseph Newton: People are lonely because they build walls
Thomas Jefferson: : When angry, count ten before you speak
Goethe: If you treat a man as he is
Thomas A. Edison: I never did anything worth doing by accident
Ralph Waldo Emerson: Life is not so short that there is always time
Thomas Hughes: Blessed are they who
Ande Gide: Assuredly all nature informs us
Bulwer Lytoon: When a person is down in the world
Thomas Paine: It is necessary to the happiness of man
Kahlil Gibran: You give but little when you give of your possessions

Dale Carnegie: One of the most tragic things I know
Dale Carnegie: Success is getting what you want
Abraham Lincoln: We are as happy as we make up our minds to be
Sir James M. Barrie: The secret of happiness is not in doing what
Solon: If all men were to bring their miseries together
Samuel Johnson: We cannot tell the precise moment when friend
George Washington: A slender acquaintance with the world must
Sidney Skolsky: Kindness is one thing
Gilbert Keith Chesterton: Don't ever take a fence down until you
Ralph Waldo Emerson: Happiness adds and multiplies

Cicero: Kindness is produced by kindness
Cicero: If we lose affection and kindness from our lire
Henry David Thoreau: What wealth it is to have such friends
Wm. Wordsworth: The best part of a good man's life
John Greenleaf Whittier: His daily prayer far better
Henry Wadsworth Longfellow: The Arrow and The Song
Robert Louise Stevenson: A friend is a present you give yourself
Anna Holden King: Growing friendship..is like a garden
Byron: Friendship is love without its wings
Benjamin Franklin: Happiness consists more

Sheryl Condie: A friend is someone you can be alone with
Richard Le Gallienne; I Meant To Do My work Today
Ah Foo Lin: Good-by..There is a word of grief
Charles Hanson Towne: Around The Corner I have a friend
David O. McKay: Ten Rules For Happiness

(Continued)

J. W. Foley: Good morning, brother Sunshine
Basil: Goodness..a good deed is never lost
Goethe: Requisites for Contented Living
Mark Twain: Kindness is a language
Abraham Lincoln: Die when I may

Henry Ward Beecher: Do not keep the alabaster boxes
W. H. Burleigh: There never was a day
C. Simmons: He who wants to do a great deal
St. Francis-Assisi: A Simple Prayer
Aristotle: Happiness itself is sufficient excuse.
Ali Ben Abau Taleb; He who has a thousand friends.
Helen Keller: When one door of happiness closes
Priscilla Leonard: The Two Seekers
Leo Tolstoy: The King and The Shirt
Palmer Muntz: The Praying Hands

James W. Foley: Drop a Pebble In The Water
Adapted by LWH In each one of us probably there is a thorn
Sam Walter Foss: The House By The Side of the Road
Homer: The House By The side of the Road
Sir Walter Foss: There are Hermit souls that live
Walter A Gresham: Crowded ways of life
Madeline S Bridges: There are loyal hearts
Ralph Waldo Emerson: Life is short
Robert Lewis Stevenson: There is no duty we so much underrate

Section 13: **Unknown**   Happiness, Friendship, Kindness

Kindness is like fresh-fallen snow
The greatest gifts you'll ever give
The grand essentials of happiness are
A man that hath friends
Don't expect to enjoy the cream of life
Friendship consists of forgetting
Kindness: I have wept in the night
Much happiness is overlooked because
Happiness is like jam
A friend is one who knows all about you

The finest kind of friendship is between
Some people come into our lives
A friend is a jewel that shines
My Friend..It is my joy in life to find
A friend: Of all the treasures one can find
One never knows how far a word of kindness goes
With kindness you can give
A friend is a person or something that likes you
Touching shoulders: There's a comforting thought
Important words: I am proud of you\

Crossing Paths with you
Don't walk in front of me,
Look Up and not down
Happiness does not come from doing easy work
Can you say in parting with the day
In exact proportion as you give
Silent Friendship That friendship runs too deep for
A favorite Recipe: Take a cup of Kindness
The Heart of Friendship: Here's to the heart
A Friend: If I could find a friend today

They planted a Seed in my heart
Story: The Old Fisherman
A Rose, a Twig and A Lily
We can complain because roses
Lincoln and The Birds

Section 14 **Authors** Life, Talents, Time, Values

Samuel Johnson: The business of life is to go forward
George W. Hegel: Life has value only when
John Lyly: The measure of life
Publius Syrus: To do two things at once
Seneca: Life is amply long for him
Mark Twain: Endeavor to so live
Sir Walter Scott: A sound head, an honest heart
Thomas Edison Everything comes to him
Stephen Grellet: Do It Now: I expect to pass through this world but
Ralph Waldo Emerson: Life consists in what

Shakespeare: All the world's a stage
Henry Wadsworth Longfellow: What is time: The shadow on
Anna R. Lindsay: The question of life is not..how much time have
Spanish Proverb: Manana is often the busiest day
Plato: Nothing is more unworthy of a wise man
John Burroughs: I still find each day too short
Benjamin Franklin: Doth thou love life
Ralph Waldo Emerson: This time, like all times is
Charles Darwin: A man who dares to waste one hour
Jonathan swift: May you live all the days of your life.

Charles R. Skinner: Do It Now..If you have hard work to do
Frances S. Osgood: Little Things: Little drops of water
Pubilus: Learn to see in another's calamity
Samuel A. Eliot: My father early gave me to understand
James I. Holt As I sit alone reflecting
Walter De La Mare: Time is a childhood's leaden wings
Ralph Waldo Emerson: Make the most of yourself
Henry David Thoreau: He went to live on the edge of a pond
Ralph Waldo Emerson: For every minute you are angry
Henry David Thoreau: It is something to be able to paint

Abraham Lincoln: The best thing about the future is
Justice Cardozo: We are what we believe we are
Henry David Thoreau: As if you could kill time
Benjamin Franklin: Dost thou love life?
Horace Mann: Lost, yesterday, somewhere between sunrise

(Continued)

Dante: To men prepared,
St. Augustine: By and By never comes
Francis Bacon: That which is past and gone
Will Rogers: Don't let yesterday use up too much of today
Henry Van Dyke: Use what talents you possess

Walt Whitman: To me every hour of the day
Plutarch: The whole life of man
Henry David Thoreau: Our life is frittered away by detail
John D. Rockefeller Jr: .I believe in the supreme worth of
Edgar A. Guest: Life is a gift to be used
Robert Browning: If you can sit at set of sun
Plautus: To mean well is nothing
Edward E. Hale: Let the scroll fill as it may
Arthur Brisbane: Don't waste time..

Robert J. Burdette: There are two days in the week
Ernest Hemingway: There are some things which cannot
Plutarch: Socrates thought that if all our misfortunes
Ecclesiastes 3: 1-8: To everything there is a season

Section 14 **Unknown**   Life Talents, Time, Values

An old man living alone
Life is not complex
If the end of life is to enjoy live
Life is learning
A good reputation
Do not put off living today
Life is a grindstone
Yesterday is a history
Life is not a goblet
Why is there never enough time

I have given you life-now make the most of it
Life itself can't bring you joy
Life is God's gift to you
Life is a road of trials
The highest of all arts is the art of living well
Many of us look for the time
It is better to be right and stand alone
Driftwood: It is not the seconds
A diamond cannot be polished
The supply of time is a daily miracle

What the future has in store for you
Yesterday is a cancelled check
Today is the day to make memories
Lost..A precious moment set with golden opportunities
As a man thinketh in his heart
Is life worth living
Know this that every soul is free
I Wish: I wish there was some wonderful place
A man's worth is determined by what he accomplishes
The beauty seen is partly in

Life wasn't meant to be lived
Man's mind is like a garden
The Touch of the Master's Hand
Frowns: If you frown at life as you go your way
Twelve Things to Remember

(Continued)

It is a good thing to have money
If you want to make an easy job seem mighty
We live in the present
What is Life to you
The loom of time

Life's Lesson: Learn to make the most of life
The River Time
When I have time
Today: Upon the threshold of today
The Best Things In Life Are Free
One solitary Life
Time is slow when we are young
Beethoven's Moonlight Sonata
The Lord Had a Job for me to do
A Piece Of Clay..

Life is largely what we make it
The clock of life is wound but once
Values of Life. supposing today were your last day on earth
How Do You Live Your Dash?
The Wrong Way: I'll go where you want me to do dear Lord
This New Day: is time to spend exactly as I choose
Then I Awoke: And in my dream
Time: The most priceless
May You Have: Enough

Section 15 **Author**   Love, Sharing, Service, Sacrifice

Thomas A. Kempis: Love is a great thing
Albert Einstein: Only a life lived to others is a life worth
George Eliot: What do we live for if not to make life less
J. Petit: We tire of those pleasures we take
Edwin Markham: There is a destiny that makes us brothers

Matt 20:27 And whosoever will be chief among you
George McDonald: In giving a man receives more than he
Edwin Markham: He drew a circle
Henry Van Dyke: Love is not getting but giving
Phillips Brooks: The truest help we can render

John 15:13
Francis W. Bourdillon: The mind has a thousand eyes
Mosiah 2: 21-22
Goethe: True Rest: Res is not quitting
Will Allen Dromgoole: The Bridge Builder

Wilfred A. Peterson: The art of love is God at work
Henry Abbey: What do we Plant
Washington Gladden: O Master, let me walk with thee
Whitney Montgomery: I knelt to pray when day was done
Albert Einstein: It's high time that the ideal of success

Roy Popkin: Night Watch..A nurse
John Ruskin: When love and skill work together
Thomas Moore: My favorite love story is also a true one.
Galen Drake: The Experience of Thomas Moore
Harry E. Fosdick: Two Seas In Palestine

Ladies Home Journal: What The Spirit of Sunshine Means
Lim Sian Tek: The Legend of The Big Bell

Section 15 **Unknown** Love, Sharing, Service, Sacrifice

Kindness: The greatest gifts you'll ever give
If you're not satisfied with your lot in life
A bell is no bell

Show you Care" Why wait till tomorrow
Let Me Be a Little Kinder
I'll go, I'll do, I'll Say

The following inscriptions on the tombstones
Footprints: One night a man had a dream
A Plea: God grant me the strength to do some needed service

A Closing Thought: Did you stop to think
The Day's Results: Is anybody happier
Suppose that today were your last day on earth

My Heart Garden: The little blossom called content
Do you wish the world were better?
Do All the good you can

A closed hand cannot receive
Father Never Knew I Loved Him
Planting a Garden: Many of us love a garden

The Rich Man and the Stone
The Bridge: There was once a big turntable
Something To think About: I did a favor yesterday

I Lived Today: Let me today do something that will
You can give without loving,

Section 16: **Authors**   Choices, Thoughts, Actions, Sorrow

Henry David Thoreau: Many of the luxuries and many of
Henry W. Longfellow: Every man has his secret sorrow
George Bernard Shaw: Better keep yourself clean
Japanese Proverb: The reputation of a thousand years
Frances W. Bourdillon: Upon the valley's lap
B.C. Forbes: Your success depends upon you
James L. Phillips: You cannot help men permanently
Emily Dickinson: If I can stop one hart from breaking
Henry Fosdick: While each of us..has depressed hours
C. Simmons: He who wants to do a great deal of good at

Joshua 24:15 Choose you this day whom ye will serve.
Ralph Waldo Emerson: Never lose an opportunity of seeing
Norman Vincent Peal: We do not fully comprehend
Matt: 5:9 Blessed are the peacemakers.
Carlyle: Silence is the element in which great things fashion
Edwin Markham: At the heart of the cyclone tearing the sky
Theodore E. Curtis: I wander throught the still of night,
Lindsay R. Curtis: We are allowed a choice at every turn of
Henry W. Longfellow: For time will teach thee soon the truth
Boree: A sound discrection is not so much indicated

Cicero:For how many things
John Lock The actions of men are the best interpreters
Sir Phillip Sidney: They are never alone that are accompanied
Latin Proverb: He who restrains his anger
John C. Metcalfe: PORCH SWING: I cannot think of anything.
Adelaide A. Proctor: The Lost Chord
John 16:33 These things I have spoken

Robert Browning Hamilton: Along The Road: I walked a mile
Matthew 5: 44 : But I say unto you, love your enemies
Ella Wheeler Wilcox: You can Never Tell when you send a
William George Jordan: Man has two creators
Matt 22:40
Barnacles: Church News, Deseret News
Leo Tolstoy: Equal Inheritance

16 Author **Unknown** Choices, Thoughts, Actions, Sorrow

If we Have Not Peace within ourselves
You live a long time with your memories
There is no pleasure in life

Repentance becomes more difficult as the sin is more willfull
Neglect of opportunity in holy things
Each day is like a clean new page

The fundamental virtue of free agency
Silence is sometimes an evidence of great courage
That's Me All Over: If I could live my life again

If you don't know where you are going
The saddest words of tongue or pen
Our thoughts are blue prints of what we propose to do.

He who chooses the beginning of a road chooses the place to
The Two Words: one day a harsh word,
Men are Sometimes just like Trees

The Only Way: And if the road were easy,
I have Found Today: I've shut the door on yesterday
Watch Your thoughts they become your words

How Many Hurts: Suppose, said I, you chanced to see
The Joy of Living: If nobody smiled and nobody cheered
There is an old old story

Choose Ye This Day
The Holy City
Beware: A Chinese legend describes
A bend in the road is not the end of the road

Section 17 **Authors**:   Teacher, Teaching, Education

Greek: If a teacher influences but one
Ralph Waldo Emerson: The creation of a thousand forests
Seneca: As long as you live...keep learning how to live
Herbert Hoover: To the three R's
Confucius: He who learns but does not think
Karl G. Measer: If a carpenter, or a black smith
Aristole: All who have meditated on the art
Proverbs 4:7 Get wisdom
Henry David Thoreau: How many a man has dated and
James Bryce: When you find that a book is poor

Strickland Gillilan: You may have tangible wealth
Schweitzer: No ray of sunshine is ever lost
D&C 88: 118 Seek ye out of the best books
Mary McLeod Bethune: Invest in a human soul
Proverbs 3:13-14 Happy is the man that findeth wisdom
Chinese Proverb: Learning is a treasure which will follow its
Socrates: A child cannot be taught
Will Rogers Everybody is ignorant Seneca: As long as you live
Dr. Nicholas Butler: There are many things that go
Derek Bok: If you think education is expensive

John Dewey: Education is growth
Thomas Watson: Wisdom is the power
Bruce B. Clark: Ignorance is dangerous
Bertrand Russell: Education ought to foster the wish for truth
B.F. Skinner: Education is not just in the filling of a pail
G.M. Trevelyan: Education has produced a vast population
Will Durant: Knowledge is the eye of desire
Plato: If a man neglects education
Mark Twain: The man who does not read
Galileo: You cannot teach a man anything

Galileo: Education is learning the rules
Theodore Roosevelt: To educate a man
John Ruskin: The object of true education
Edward S. Ufford: He who knows not and know not
Confucius: Ignorance is the night of the mind

(Continued)

Euripides: Who so neglects learning
Galileo: That which we learn pleasantly we retain
Ralph Waldo Emerson: What school, college or lecture
Andrew Lang: I'd leave all the hurry
Robert Louis Stevenson: The Land of Story Books

Samuel Johnson: It is no matter what you teach them
Helen Keller: I have walked with people whose eyes are full
J. Karl Wood : First Day of School
Hattie Rose Hall: Two Temples
Leo Tolstoy: The Learned Son

Ralph Waldo Emmerson: Character is higher than intellect
James Bryant Conant: The primary concern of American
C.J. Wendell: The Unmailed Letter
Judith Swanson: From the day we entered the ninth-grade
Virginia Church: Each day I learn more than I teach.

Section 17: **Author Unknown**   Teacher, Teaching Education

Education does not commence with the alphabet
If a man neglects education
I'd laugh today, today is brief

If you graduated yesterday
The Teacher: Lord who am I
The basic ingredient of teaching

A Diamond In The Rough: is a diamond sure enough
The Light of My Love: I cannot watch you all the way
An Individual Learns best those things that he wants to learn

I saw Tomorrow passing on little children's feet
Ten Commandments for Teacher:: Thou shalt make
Sculpturing: I dreamed I stood in a studio

Section 18 **Authors**:

Confucius: A man who has committed
Benjamin Franklin: Sin is not hurtful
Henry Van Dyke: Every Task, However Simple

Alexander Pope: Teach me to feel another's woes
Charles Wagner: Bury Your Wrongs
Robert Burns: Man's Inhumanity to Man

John Greenleaf Whittier: On Rising Above The Hurt
D & C. 58:42: Behold, he who has repented of his sins
C. Maud Battersby: Evening Prayer:. If I have wounded

D&C 64: 9-11: You ought to forgive one another
Stuart Chase: In business men talk of service
Frank Cox: Mother's Forgiveness

Claremont Herald: What To Forget
Phillips Brooks: Forgiving and Forgetting
Ralph Waldo Emerson: Wrong Doings

18:**Unknown** authors   Forgiving, Tolerance, Mercy, Greed

Somebody did a golden deed
Folks and Me;;It is a funny thing but true
Forgetting: If you were busy being kind

Forgive: Do you ever stop to think
Let Each Man Learn to Know Himself
A Story To Remember: three Arabian Horsemen

Judge Not: Pray do not find fault with the man
Forgiveness is not just
I'm Going Home:

It Will Mend
Tolerance: Don't condemn a man

19: **Authors** Work, Responsibility, Leisure, Idleness, Debt

Henry David Thoreau: It is not enough to be industrious
D&C 42:42 He that is idle shall not eat the bread
Thomas Edison: I am glad the eight hour day
Sophocles: Without labor nothing prospers
Thomas Carlyle: A man without a purpose is like a ship

Seneca: Nothing is so certain as that the evils
Luc De Clapiers Vauvenarjues: the fruit derived from labor
Sir Joshua Reynolds: Simplicity is an exact medium
Galatians 6:7 Whatsoever a man soweth
Sarah A. Bolton: A victory of success is half won

Confucian Proverb: He who sits cross-legged
Ralph Waldo Emerson Life is hardly respectable
Thomas Carlyle: In idleness there is perpetual despair
Robert Lewis Stevenson: I know what happiness is
Fredick P. Latiner: The Weary wisher I wish I were a little rock

R.L. Sharpe: Each is given a bag pf tools
Socrates: He is not only idle who does nothing
George S. Hillard: The ruin of most men dates from some
Swiss Saying: With one foot in, With one footout
Mark8:36: For what shall it profit a man

Benjamin Franklin: Getting in debt is getting into a tanglesome
Proverbs 22: 7 The rich ruleth over the poor
Nathaniel Howe: The way to be nothing is to do nothing
F.L. Emerson: I'm a good believer in luck
St. Augustine: Faith is to believe what we do not see

Benjamin Franklin: When men are employed, they are best
Ralph Waldo Emerson: In every variety of human employment
Thomas Carlyle: Idleness alone is without hope
Robert J. Burdette: Remember My Son you have to work
Johann Wolfgang Von Goethe: As A Man Soweth..we must

(Continued)

George Bernard Shaw: I am of the opinion that my life
George W. Balli: How much easier our work would be if
Benjamin Franklin: Idleness make all things difficult but
Margaret E. Sangster: The Average Man..when it comes to
D.&C. 42:42 Thou shalt not be idle

Edward Gibbon: In his book Decline and fall of the
Edgar A. Guest: I Couldn't Be Done
W.H. Davies: Leisure..What is life if full of care
Nashville American: The Right Sort of Grit
Benjamin Franklin: Think what you do when you run

Benjamin Franklin: Work while it is called today,
L.W.H: The Chambered Nautilus
Oliver Wendell Holmes: The Chambered Nautilus
Theodore Roosevelt: In the battle of life it is not the
Thomas Carlyle: There is one advice I must give you.

Charles Kingsley: Thank God every morning when
Abraham Lincoln: You cannot help small men by
Juvenile Court: Open Letter To a Teen-Ager
Edgar A. Guest: Work: How do you tackle your
Plato: Nothing is more unworthy of a wise man

Robert Lewis Stevenson: When we look into the long
Don Marquis: Procrastination
Ralph Waldo Emerson:What wold be the use of immortality
Alma 34:32 This life
Confucious: When prosperity comes

Mary Singleton: Ah, All things come
Dante: To men prepared

19 **Unknown** Work, Responsibility, Leisure, Idleness, Debt

Hard work never killed a man
The average person puts only 25%
Some one's Selfish, some one's lazy
There is no shame in honorable work
My Little Place: Father, where shall I work today?

The Only Way: If the road were easy
There is a difference between sitting before the fire and
He who complains loudest about the way
A healthy person looks upon inaction
Fortune favors the best

Horse Sense: a horse can't pull while kicking
Heights of Great Men reached
Pray As though everything depends on the Lord
If you want to earn more than you get
The soul is dyed with the color of its leisure thoughts

Thems that understand interest receives it
He who owes another does not altogether own himself
My Friend have you heard of The town of Yawn
Do It Now: If you've got a job to do, Do It Now!
Work: Don't be afraid of work

Tomorrow; She is going to be all
Managing Money: Anyone who has bogged down in
A Bride to be would do well to ask herself
Many who blame the economy for all their financial woes
For great and low, there is but one test

She is going to be all that a mortal should be
The Wise Old Lark
Always
Finish: If a task is once begun

Section 20 **Authors**   Smiles, Laughter, Hugs, Humor

Daniel Taylor: Smile: If you chance to meet a frown
Nixon Waterman: If I knew you and you knew me
Lois de Louk: Infection: A baby smiled in its mother's face

Emily Dickinson: They may not need me, but they might.
William M. Thackeray: A good laugh is sunshine in a house.

Verna Young: Have you tried out your smile today?
Ella Wheeler Wilcox: Smile: It's easy enough to be pleasant

Ella Wheeler Wilcox: Laugh and the world laughs with you
Leo Tolstoy: Three Rolls and a Pretzel

John Godfrey Saxe: The Blind Men and the Elephant
W.D. Nesbitt: Let us Smile..The thing that goes the fartherest

Thomas Paine: I love the man that can smile in trouble
L.F. Rook: Harry's Lecture

Section 20 **Unknown** Authors Smiles, Laughter, Hugs, Humor

God gave all people in every nation
A smile is the same in any language.
A smile is a curve

Actions speak louder than words
When you meet a person without a smile
A smile increases your face value
Keep Smiling: My father smiled this morning

Hugs: it's wondrous what a hug can do
 Love Cake:
Oh! What would people do
Ma's Tools

The Bible: I found an old dusty book high
Two Little Kittens
Playing Hookey
A monkey's viewpoint

Mr. Mean-to has a comrade,
The Under Dog: I know that this world
Family Financiering: They tell me work for a dollar a day;
Dad's Old Breeches: When dad has worn his trousers out

The Hardship of accounting: Never ask of money spent
The Value of A Smile: It cost nothing
Why Laugh?
There are three kinds of people

A Young boy came home from Sunday School
A smile Says a Lot
If You Can Smile: when things go wrong
Zig Zag Children

Why People Go To Church
A Sunday Day School teacher asked the children to draw
The Two Bills